Methods of Social Work *and* Participation

Methods of Social Work *and* Participation

Dr. P. Venu Gopala Rao
Prof. Y. Ashok Kumar

ABD PUBLISHERS
Jaipur ■ New Delhi

ABD PUBLISHERS

Regd. Off. "Bony Residency", Gate No. 2
Opp. Tilak Public School, Vishweswariya Nagar,
Gopalpura Road, Jaipur - 302018, India
Ph: 0141 - 2761280, Telefax: 2761381
Email: abdpublishersjpr@gmail.com

Delhi Office: 102, 1st Floor, Satyam House,
4327/3, Ansari Road, Darya Ganj,
New Delhi - 110002, India
Ph: 011-45652440

visit us: www.oxfordbookcompany.com

Distributed By
KEYA INTERNATIONAL PRESS LLP
E-mail: keyainternationalpressllp@gmail.com

Published in India, 2026

ISBN: 9788183768481

Typeset by Shivangi Computer, Jaipur

Printed and bound in India by Thomson Press Ltd.,
New Delhi

Contents

Preface

Community practice techniques have been neglected by social work educators and authors, reflecting a lack of fit with real world practice needs. Community practice is defined as including community organizing, community development, and social planning. To sharpen the debate, the authors identify five techniques that are helpful, if not essential for community practice:

- Force Field Analysis;
- Programme Evaluation Review Technique;
- Nominal Group Technique;
- Delphi; and
- Q-Sort.

It is anticipated that this book could spark a dialogue leading ultimately to a universally accepted set of community practice techniques in social work.

This book titled "Methods of Social Work and Participation" deals with the said subject of methods of social work and social work participation in its totality. It provides readers with knowledge about volunteering, voluntary sector and NGOs and helps towards understanding the contemporary social welfare systems and civil society. An attempt is made towards understanding NGOs and their major characteristics. The ways for evolving accountability of voluntary organizations are analyzed and the contributions of NGOs to development are discussed. Modern trends in role of voluntary sector in India are described. Issues related to motivations of voluntary organizations in India are discussed. This book is user-friendly as it contains annolated Bibliography and detailed Indcx.

Major content includes: Methods of Social Work and Social Work Participation; Volunteering, Voluntary Sector and NGOs; Contemporary Social Welfare Systems and Civil Society; Towards Understanding NGOs; Major Characteristics of NGOs; Evolving Accountability of Voluntary Organisations; Contribution of NGOs to Development; Role of Voluntary Organisations in Social Development; Role of Voluntary Sector in India and Motivations of Voluntary Organisations in India etc.

—Dr. P. Venu Gopala Rao
Prof. Y. Ashok Kumar

CHAPTER 1

Methods of Social Work and Social Work Participation

> But the general welfare must restrict and regulate the exertions of the individuals, as the individuals must derive a supply of their strength from social power.
>
> —*Friedrich List*

Methods of Social Work

Social work as a profession is a product of this century. Although its roots are well established in history from the time when people 1st began to take responsibility for their neighbours through activities which were called charity, poor relief, philanthropy and social reform. Social work is to fight against Five Evils as:

1. Physical want.
2. Disease.
3. Ignorance.
4. Squalor.
5. Idleness.

Objective:

- To remove social injustice
- To relieve social injustice
- To reduce redress

- To prevent suffering
- To assist the weaker sections
- To rehabilitate the distress class people.

Major Methods of Social Work

Social Case Work

Social case work is a method which helps by counselling the individual client to effect better social relationships & a social adjustment that makes it possible him to lead a satisfying & useful life. Gordon Hamilton points out that, "The objective of case work is to administer practical services & offer counselling in such a way as to arouse & conserve psychological energies of the client activity to involve him in the use of the service towards the solution of her/his dilemma."

Social Group Work

Social group work is an activity which helps to participate in the activities of a group for their intellectual, emotional & physical growth and for the attainment of desirable goals of the groups. Group work as such as a method by which the group worker enables various types of groups to function in such a manner that both group interaction & programme activities contribute to the growth of the individual & the programme activities contribute to the growth of the individual & the achievement of desirable social goals.

Community Organisation

Community organisation is the process of planning & developing social services in order to meet the health & welfare needs of a community or larger unit. Mildred Barry says," Community organisation in social work is the process of creating & maintaining a progressively more effective adjustment between community resources & commuity welfare needs."

Social Action

It s an organised group process solving general social

problems & furthering social welfare objectives by legislative, social, health or economic progress. The term social action refers to organised & legally permitted activities designed to mobiles public opinion, legislation & public administration in favour of objectives believed to be socially desirable.

Social Welfare Research

Social welfare research systematic critically investigation of questions in the social welfare field with the purpose of yielding answares to problems of social work & of extending generally social work concept. The methods appliesd in social work research have been to a largwe extent derived grom those used in sociology & social psychology as well as in history and Anthropology.

Social Welfare Administration

Social welfare administration process is to organise & to direct a social agency. The administrative aspects of social work have to do with the organisation & management of social agencies public & private, including in those terms general administrative relationships among ubnits of the same organisation, personal problems, questions of finance & so on.

Participation and Participatory Decision Making

Participation in social science refers to different mechanisms for the public to express opinions-and ideally exert influence-regarding political, economic, management or other social decisions. Participatory decision making can take place along any realm of human social activity, including economic (i.e. participatory economics), political (i.e. participatory democracy or parpolity), management (i.e. participatory management), cultural (i.e. intercommunalism) or familial (i.e. feminism). For well-informed participation to occur, it is argued that some version of transparency, e.g. radical transparency, is necessary, but not sufficient. It has also been argued that those most affected by a decision should have the most say while those least affected would have the least say.

Objectives of Participation

Participation activities may be motivated from an administrative perspective or a citizen perspective. From the administrative viewpoint, participation can build public support for activities. It can educate the public about an agency's activities. It can also facilitate useful information exchange regarding local conditions. Furthermore, participation is often legally mandated. From the citizen viewpoint, participation enables individuals and groups to influence agency decisions in a representational manner.

Classifying Participation

Sherry Arnstein discusses eight types of participation in *A Ladder of Citizen Participation* (1969). These are broadly categorised as Nonparticipation, Tokenism, and Citizen Power. She defines citizen participation as the redistribution of power that enables the havenot citizens, presently excluded from the political and economic processes, to be deliberately included in the future. Archon Fung presents another classification of participation based on three key questions: Who is allowed to participate, and are they representative of the population? What is the method of communication or decision-making? And how much influence or authority is granted to the participation?

Personal Practice Model in Social Work

A Personal practice model (PPM) is a social work tool for understanding and linking theories to each other and to the practical tasks of social work. Muller describes the PPM as "the art and science of social work", or more prosaically, "an explicit conceptual scheme that expresses a worker's view of practice". A worker should develop a PPM pragmatically over their entire career by reflecting on, and the absorption of, a variety of sources. They are an important basis for the delivery of good practice and the evaluation of such. Bowles, Collingridge, Curry and Valentine stress the importance of deriving the guidelines for good practice from a text such as the Australian Association of Social Workers Code of Ethics. As the name implies, they are fundamentally personal and idiosyncratic, and to be effective, they must be rationally constructed, by a self-conscious worker. Fook identifies the need to maintain "a broader vision of the mission of social work" to transcend everyday workplace distractions. Muller describes the dimensions and sub-dimension of a PPM, outlined below. It contains all elements of social work theory, linking what Payne describes as the three tiers; models of practice, explanatory theory and world perspectives.

REFERENCES

Amrita Basu, *Two facts of Protest: Contrasting Modes of Women's Activism in India* (Berkeley: University of California Press, 1992), p. 16.

Bharat Jhunjhunwala, 'Voluntary work as countervailing power", *Economic and Political Weekly* 21, 1986, p. 599.

D.L. Sheth and Harsh Sethi, 'The NGO sector in India: Historical context and current discourse', *Voluntas* 2, 1991, p. 51.

Devaki Jain, 'Voluntary agencies and their role', *Mian Express* (New Delhi), 1 July 1985.

Dinesh Shah, Voluntary agencies in the seventh plan', *Voluntary Action* 27, nos 9-10, 1985, p. 259.

E. Fama and M. Jensen, 'Separation of ownership and control', *Journal of Law and Economics* 26,1994. pp 301-26.

H. Hansmann, The role of non-profit enterprise', *Yale Law Journal* 89, 1979-80, pp 835-901.

Harsh Sethi, 'Groups in a new politics of transformation', n. 7.

John Clark, *Democratising Development: The Role of Voluntary Organisations* London: Earthscan Publications, 1991).

David C. Korten, 'Third generation NGO strategoes: A key to people-centered development", *World Development* 15, 1987, pp 145-59.

Korten, 'The role of nongovernmental organisations in development: Changing patterns and perspectives' in Samuel Paul and Arturo Israel (eds), *Nongovernmental Organisations and the World Bank: Cooperation far Development* (Washington, D.C: The World Bank, 1991).

Harsh Sethi, 'Groups in a new politics of transformation', n. 14, pp 305-16.

John R. Wood, 'Extra-parliamentary opposition in India: An analysis of populist agitations in Gujarat and Bihar', *Pacific Affairs* 48, 1975, p. 327.

K.M. *Sen, Hinduism* (Baltimore: Penguin Books, 1961), pp 23-24.

Karl Marx, 'Theses on Feuerbach' in Eugene Kamenka (ed.), *The Portable Karl Marx* (New York: Viking, 1983), p. 158.

Leslie J. Calman, *Toward Empowerment: Women and Movement Politics in India* (Boulder, CO: Westview, 1992), pp. 21-46.

Myron Weiner, 'Struggle against power: Notes on Indian political behaviour', *World Politics 7,* 1956, pp 393-96.

Myron Weiner, 'The Indian paradox: Violent social conflict and democratic polities' in S.N. Eisenstadt (ed.), *Democracy and Modernity* (Leiden: EJ. Brill, 1991), pp 69-85.

Pandey, *Community Action,* n.5, pp 249-50.

Prakash Karat, 'Action groups/voluntary organisarons: A factor in imperialist strategy', *The Marxist,* April-June, 1984, pp 19-54.

Rajni Kothari, 'NGOs, the state and world capitalism', *Economic and Political Weekly* 21, 1986, p. 2178.

S.L. Sharma, 'Social action groups as harbingers of silent revolution, *Economic and Political Weekly* 27, 1992, pp 2557-61.

Smitu Kothari, 'Social movements and the redefinition of democracy' in Philip Oldenburg (ed.), *India Briefing, 1993* (Boulder, CO: Westview Press, 1993), p. 142.

Stanley A. Kochanek, *Business and Politics in India* (Berkeley: University of California Press, 1974 p. 64.

CHAPTER 2

Volunteering, Voluntary Sector and NGOs

> A new sense of shared international responsibility is unmistakable in the voices of the United Nations and its agencies, and in the civil society of thousands of supra-national NGOs.
>
> —*John Charles Polany*

Introduction

The main feature of this sector is the lack of profit and the dedication to a particular cause. The voluntary sector in the UK currently has a turnover of £20 billion and continues to grow. The type of experience that can be gained is very varied. There are many opportunities ranging from working in an administrative or commercial capacity such as in marketing to practical work such as environmental field projects, campaigning, fundraising or shop-work. Some volunteering opportunities require people to offer individual support to groups or people such as those with illnesses or disabilities.

Benefits of Volunteering

- *Learning new skills* – these can include practical skills as well as 'soft' skills such as communication, time management and problem solving.
- *Experience* – you can gain valuable experience for an area that you would like a career in, for example teaching, PR or social work. The same is true if you

need experience to be considered for a vocational course. Volunteering also offers you a 'safe' environment in which to test out certain career areas to see if they are something that you wish to pursue.

- *Meeting new people*-volunteering allows you to meet people outwith your own social circle. These can be students from other degree courses and universities, people in a different age group from you and people from different backgrounds. It can be a chance to find out more about the community you live in outside of university. In these situations you will no doubt form friendships but you will also find this an opportunity for you to network now and in the future.
- *Giving something back*-for some people volunteering is entirely altruistic.
- *Learning more about a cause*-if there is a cause that you have a special affinity with, then through volunteering with a relevant organisation you can learn more about it.
- *Improving confidence and feeling of self-worth*-being an important part of a team or being highly valued by an individual you are working with can do wonders for your self-esteem.

It is important to remember that all types of employers view volunteering as just as valuable, and in some cases more valuable than, paid work. If you are interested in making a career in the voluntary sector see the section on Charities and Voluntary Organisations and also Development Work and Emergency Planning.

Thinking about Becoming a Volunteer

What's in it for me?

- a sense of personal fulfilment?
- an opportunity to 'give something back'?
- involvement in the community?
- the chance to meet new people?
- to acquire new skills?

- the opportunity to explore new areas of work; test out suitability and commitment before making career decisions?
- necessary pre-course experience?
- enhancing your CV?

Don't be surprised if your reasons are partly altruistic and partly self-beneficial. Voluntary organisations are well aware that volunteers need to gain something for themselves from the experience.

What Can I Offer?

- *Personal qualities*-projects seeking volunteers tend to value enthusiasm, new ideas and hard work more than specific skills. People skills — cheerfulness, patience and understanding — are most important.
- *Expertise*-particular abilities will always be welcomed. Conservation projects appeal to those with practical or technical skills. Teaching, advisory and counselling activities demand high levels of communication skills. Being able to drive could be a useful asset.
- *Affinity*-support for a cause, concern for a special project or group of people or sharing the aims, objectives and values of a specific organisation could lend support to your desire to be a volunteer.
- *Time commitment*-how much time can you realistically spare? Some voluntary projects may only need you on an 'as and when available' basis. Others, particularly when working in a supporting or teaching capacity or when specific training is offered, will look for regular and sustained involvement. You may need to agree a mutual trial period with the voluntary organisation.

Possible Downsides

It is also important to think about what some people regard as the more negative side of volunteering. For some the lack of contact with the people you are helping can be dispiriting, for example if you are working in the UK office of an overseas development agency. You also have to think about the work you will be doing and whether you will find it too emotionally distressing or stressful. You are welcome to discuss any aspects of volunteering with a careers adviser.

Volunteering in the UK

Types of Work

- *Social care*-Typical roles include: advice worker (e.g. advising on consumer, legal and employment issues); drug user support worker; kitchen assistant for homeless people; project organiser. (N.B. Information on working in social care can be found in the careers websites section under *Social, Guidance and Community Work (B)).*
- *Environment and Animals*-Typical roles include: conservation volunteer; researcher; animal fosterer; farming assistant; rescue worker; fundraiser. (N.B. Information on working with the environment and animals can be found in the careers websites section under *Natural Resources and the Environment (R)* and *Animal and Plant Resources (S)).*
- *Education and Youth Work*-Typical roles include: literacy/numeracy tutor; IT tutor; Girl Guides/Scout leader; youth leader; student tutor in schools. (N.B. Information on careers working in education and youth work can be found in the careers websites section under *Education (A)* and *Social, Guidance and Community Work (B)).*
- *Children and Families*-Typical roles include: befriender; childsitter; telephone counsellor; crèche worker; mentor. (N.B. Information on careers working with children and families can be found in the careers websites section under *Social, Guidance and Community Work (B)).*
- *Health*-Typical roles include: hospital "buddy" (i.e. providing friendship to people in long term care); information officer; providing therapeutic care (e.g.

massages for those in hospitals, hospices and respite care); ward helpers; care worker. (N.B. Information on careers in health can be found in the careers websites section under *Health Care and Psychology (C)).*

- *Arts, Sports and Culture*-Typical roles include: music group facilitator; choir organiser; crafts group support assistant; historic house guide; lifeguard; sports coach; referee. (N.B. Information on arts, sports and culture can be found in the careers websites section under *Publishing, Media and Performing Arts (Y), Leisure, Sport and Tourism (F)* and *Information, Patents and Heritage Management (W)).*
- *Equality*-Typical roles include: web designer; committee member; administrator.
- *Community Development*-Typical roles include: community radio staff; assistant in children and women's groups; journalist (community magazines/newspapers).
- *Working with the Elderly*-Typical roles include: IT teacher; mini bus driver; café assistant; social club helper; day care assistant.

Issues to Consider

Before you get started you should be clear about how much time you can devote. If you are studying you should remember that your workload will vary throughout the year and you do not want to disappoint anyone when you are under pressure and are unable to volunteer. If you find an opportunity that you are interested in you should find out as much as you can about it. Most projects will have a volunteer manager or coordinator and they should be able to give you a good explanation of what your role will be. If you are keen to volunteer in a different part of the UK, there are plenty of residential placements that exist. The length of these range from a week to a year. Find out in advance as much as you can about what the placement will involve so that things like the standard of accommodation or number of hours you are requested to work don't come as a surprise when you get there!

Volunteering in the Edinburgh Area

Here are some starting points for finding out about the huge variety of opportunities that exist to volunteer in Edinburgh:

- *SAGE*-any volunteering opportunities that the Careers Service is made aware of are advertised on SAGE. SAGE is updated daily so you should check it regularly.
- *Student Volunteer Centre*-provides information and advice for University of Edinburgh students (and staff) who are considering volunteering in Edinburgh, the UK or abroad. The centre can also help student **voluntary groups.** They are based at 5/1 Bristo Square and are open for you just to drop in.
- *Volunteer Centre Edinburgh*-acts as a placement and advice service for volunteers in Edinburgh. Their website contains a searchable database of current opportunities.
- *Student Societies*-many student societies are involved in local volunteering projects.
- *LEAPS (Lothians Equal Access Programme for Schools)*-aims to increase participation in higher education amongst students from non-traditional backgrounds through a programme that includes a pre-application interview and enquiry service, school and university-based events and an eight-week summer school for school leavers. Student volunteers are welcome and the experience is especially useful if you are thinking about going into a teaching/social work career.
- *Power of 5*-this website is aimed at 16-25 year olds in Edinburgh who want to find out more information about volunteering. The site has case studies of current volunteers and details of how to get involved in volunteering.

Volunteering Overseas

Benefits

Volunteering overseas has all the benefits of volunteering in the UK as well as providing the opportunity to experience a new culture and country. Many volunteering placements have the option of travelling after the placement has ended. A large number of placements take place in rural locations and provide you with the opportunity to see areas off the beaten track. By working and/or living with local people you will learn a lot about the culture of a country and, potentially, a new language. You should bear in mind that it will take you longer to organise a volunteer placement overseas than it would in the UK so make sure that you allow yourself enough time.

Types of Work

What you could be doing overseas is very varied. The main types of volunteer work that students and graduates are involved in are:

- *Conservation*-projects include monitoring species populations and habitats on land and in the sea. Some projects also include an educational element, for example you would teach the importance of conservation to local people. (N.B. Information on careers in conservation can be found in the careers websites section under *Natural Resources and the Environment (R)).*
- *Construction*-building places that will benefit whole communities, such as schools, community centres and houses. (N.B. Information on careers in construction can be found in the careers websites section under *Construction, Civil Engineering and Property (Q)).*
- *Teaching/Education*-this includes teaching English, sports and music to young children through to adults. Health education is also a popular area to volunteer in and can often be done in conjunction with a teaching placement. (N.B. Information on careers in education can be found in the careers websites section under *Education (A)).*
- *Youth Work*-includes working with children in orphanages, children with disabilities and street

children. (N.B. Information on youth work can be found in the careers websites section under *Social, Guidance and Community Work (B)).*

- *Social and Community Work*-working in a community, sometimes with specific groups, such as women, to promote awareness of a wide range of issues. (N.B. Information on social and community work can be found in the careers websites section under *Social, Guidance and Community Work (B)).*
- *Healthcare*-using skills already gained in healthcare in projects overseas. Medical students early on in their studies can be involved in some projects. (N.B. Information on healthcare can be found in the careers websites section under *Health Care and Psychology (C)).*

Cost and Length of Placement

You will find that most overseas placements will require you to pay something towards taking part (sometimes called a 'donation'). This is usually to cover things like accommodation, food, travel within the country and insurance (n.b. flights aren't always included in the cost). Some placements can be quite pricey so it makes sense to 'shop around' and find exactly where your money would be going. How much you pay is usually dependent on how long you intend to be volunteering for. The length of placements varies, from a week to a year. It is unusual to find placements that last longer than twelve months and those that do are usually for specialist roles such as medics and engineers. It is the policy of the Careers Service not to advertise placements on SAGE where costs seem excessive compared to other similar placements. However, we can take no responsibility for organisations, the work or the costs involved.

Research and Fund-raising

Research the organisation: Before signing up for anything it is essential that you have fully researched the organisation and what you will actually be doing once you are overseas. You should read Some Basic Questions to Ask Before Accepting an Overseas Placement. Try to get in contact with previous volunteers and don't just rely on information in promotional literature or on websites. Some voluntary organisations hold information events where previous volunteers are on hand to talk about their experiences. Find out how much support you will have from the organisation when you are overseas and what they do to help volunteers if there is an emergency. It is worth thinking about whether your placement will result in a local person being denied a job.

Most organisations will strive to avoid this happening. The amount that you require for your placement will probably mean that you will have to do some fund-raising. Voluntary organisations should be able to help you with fund-raising by providing ideas and suggesting possible sources of funds. You may find it useful to look at our funding information. We also keep lots of helpful reference books which relate to funding.

We also have the programme FunderFinder on our PCs, which can help you identify suitable potential sources of financial help. The University's Scholarships and Student Finance office may also be able to help. How you find the funds to be able to do your placement is very much part of the whole experience and you will find that you will gain a wide range of valuable skills from this exercise alone. It is essential that you allow enough time for your fund-raising.

Emergency/Relief Work

Many people are attracted to the idea of being involved in emergency/relief work overseas. While this is quite understandable it is important to bear in mind a couple of points. This type of work is usually carried out by highly qualified specialists which the country in crisis either does not have or does not have enough of. This will include professions such as firefighters, engineers and healthcare professionals. Even if there is a need for semi-skilled or unskilled workers it is preferable that these positions are filled by local people. If you are interested in this kind of work it may be useful to have a look at the RedR website. RedR is an international organisation which assists frontline organisations with finding personnel.

Non-Governmental Organisations (NGOs)

Non-governmental organisation is a term that has become widely accepted as referring to a legally constituted, non-governmental organisation created by natural or legal persons with no participation or representation of any government. In the cases in which NGOs are funded totally or partially by governments, the NGO maintains its non-governmental status and excludes government representatives from membership in the organisation. Unlike the term *intergovernmental organisation*, "non-governmental organisation" is a term in general use but is not a legal definition. In many jurisdictions these types of organisation are defined as "civil society organisations" or referred to by other names. The number of internationally operating NGOs is estimated at 40,000. National numbers are even higher: Russia has 277,000 NGOs. India is estimated to have between 1 million and 2 million NGOs.

National NGOs go back to antiquity. International non-governmental organisations have a history dating back to at least 1839. Rotary, later Rotary International, was founded in 1905. It has been estimated that by 1914 there were 1083 NGOs. International NGOs were important in the anti-slavery movement and the movement for women's suffrage, and reached a peak at the time of the World Disarmament Conference. However, the phrase "non-governmental organisation" only came into popular use with the establishment of the United Nations Organisation in 1945 with provisions in Article 71 of Chapter 10 of the United Nations Charter for a consultative role for organisations which are neither governments nor member states—see Consultative Status. The definition of "international NGO" (INGO) is first given in resolution 288 (X) of ECOSOC on February 27, 1950: it is defined as "any international organisation that is not founded by an international treaty". The vital role of NGOs and other "major groups" in sustainable development was recognised in Chapter 27 of Agenda 21, leading to intense arrangements for a consultative relationship between the United Nations and non-governmental organisations. Rapid development of the non-governmental sector occurred in western countries as a result of the processes of restructurisation of the welfare state.

Further globalisation of that process occurred after the fall of the communist system and was an important part of the Washington consensus. Globalisation during the 20th century gave rise to the importance of NGOs. Many problems could not be solved within a nation. International treaties and international organisations such as the World Trade Organisation were perceived as being too centred on the interests of capitalist enterprises. Some argued that in an attempt to counterbalance this trend, NGOs have developed to emphasize humanitarian issues, developmental aid and sustainable development.

A prominent example of this is the World Social Forum which is a rival convention to the World Economic Forum held annually in January in Davos, Switzerland. The fifth World Social Forum in Porto Alegre, Brazil, in January 2005 was attended by representatives from more than 1,000 NGOs. Some have argued that in forums like these, NGOs take the place of what should belong to popular movements of the poor. Others argue that NGOs are often imperialist in nature, that they sometimes operate in a racialised manner in dominant countries, and that they fulfil a similar function to that of the clergy during the high colonial era. The philosopher Peter Hallward argues that they are an aristocratic form of politics. However, this philosophy would suggest that organisations of indigenous peoples are not represented, which is untrue. Whatever the case, NGO transnational networking is now extensive.

Types of NGOs

Apart from "NGO", often alternative terms are used as for example: independent sector, volunteer sector, civil society, grassroots organisations, transnational social movement organisations, private voluntary organisations, self-help organisations and non-state actors (NSA's). Non-governmental organisations are a heterogeneous group. A long list of acronyms has developed around the term “NGO”.

These Include

- *CSO:* short for civil society organisation;
- *DONGO:* Donor Organised NGO;
- *ENGO:* short for environmental NGO, such as Global 2000;
- *GONGO:* are government-operated NGOs, which may have been set up by governments to look like NGOs in order to qualify for outside aid or promote the interests of the government in question;
- *INGO:* stands for international NGO; Oxfam is an international NGO
- *QUANGO:* are quasi-autonomous non-governmental organisations, such as the International Organisation for Standardisation (ISO).

(The ISO is actually not purely an NGO, since its membership is by nation, and each nation is represented by what the ISO Council determines to be the ‘most broadly representative’ standardisation body of a nation. That body might itself be a nongovernmental organisation; for example, the United States is represented in ISO by the American National Standards Institute, which is independent of the federal government. However, other countries can be represented by national governmental agencies; this is the trend in Europe.)

- *TANGO:* short for technical assistance NGO;
- *GSO:* Grassroots Support Organisation
- *MANGO:* short for market advocacy NGO.

There are also numerous classifications of NGOs. The typology the World Bank uses divides them into Operational and Advocacy: The primary purpose of an operational NGO is the design and implementation of development-related projects. One frequently used categorisation is the division into *relief-oriented* versus *development-oriented* organisations; they can also be classified according to whether they stress service delivery or participation; or whether they are religious or secular; and whether they are more public or private-oriented. Operational NGOs can be community-based, national or international. The primary purpose of an Advocacy NGO is to defend or promote a specific cause. As opposed to operational project management, these organisations typically try to raise awareness, acceptance and knowledge by lobbying, press work and activist events. USAID refers to NGOs as *private voluntary organisations*. However many scholars have argued that this definition is highly problematic as many NGOs are in fact state and corporate funded and managed projects with professional staff. NGOs exist for a variety of reasons, usually to further the political or social goals of their members or funders. Examples include improving the state of the natural environment, encouraging the observance of human rights, improving the welfare of the disadvantaged, or representing a corporate agenda. However, there are a huge number of such organisations and their goals cover a broad range of political and philosophical positions. This can also easily be applied to private schools and athletic organisations.

Methods

NGOs vary in their methods. Some act primarily as lobbyists, while others primarily conduct programmes and activities. For instance, an NGO such as Oxfam, concerned with poverty alleviation, might provide needy people with the equipment and skills to find food and clean drinking water, whereas an NGO like the FFDA helps through investigation and documentation of human rights violations and provides legal assistance to victims of human rights abuses. Others, such as Afghanistan Information Management Services, provide specialised technical products and services to support development activities implemented on the ground by other organisations.

Public Relations

Non-governmental organisations need healthy relationships with the public to meet their goals. Foundations and charities use sophisticated public relations campaigns to raise funds and employ standard lobbying techniques with governments. Interest groups may be of political importance because of their ability to influence social and political outcomes.

Volunteering

Volunteering is the practice of people working on behalf of others or a particular cause without payment for their time and services. Volunteering is generally considered an altruistic activity, intended to promote good or improve human quality of life, but people also volunteer for their own skill development, to meet others, to make contacts for possible employment, to have fun, and a variety of other reasons that could be considered self-serving. Volunteering takes many forms and is performed by a wide range of people. Many volunteers are specifically trained in the areas they work in, such as medicine, education, or emergency rescue. Other volunteers serve on an as-needed basis, such as in response to a natural disaster or for a beach-cleanup.

Social Capital

The *social capital* represented by volunteering plays a key role in economic regeneration. Where poverty is endemic to an area, poor communities lack friends and neighbours able to help. This, voluntary mutual aid or self-help is an important safety net. This model works well within a state because there is a national solidarity in times of adversity and more prosperous groups will usually make sacrifices for the benefit of those in need.

Skills-based Volunteering

Skills-based volunteering refers to volunteering in which the volunteer is specifically trained in the area they are volunteering in. This is in contrast to traditional volunteering, where specific training is not required. The average hour of traditional volunteering is valued by the Independent Sector at between $18–20 an hour. Skills-based volunteerism is valued at $40–500 an hour depending on the market value of the time.

Virtual-Volunteering

Virtual volunteering, also sometimes called as eVolunteering, online volunteering or micro-volunteering, is a term describing a volunteer who completes tasks, in whole or in part, offsite from the organisation being assisted, using the Internet and a home, school, tele centre or work computer or other Internet-connected device, such as a PDAs or smart phone. Virtual volunteering is also known as cyber service, tele mentoring, and tele tutoring, and various other names. Virtual volunteering is similar to tele commuting, except that, instead of online employees who are paid, these are online volunteers who are not paid.

Environmental-Volunteering

Environmental volunteering refers to volunteers who contribute towards environmental management. Volunteers conduct a range of activities including environmental monitoring, ecological restoration such as re-vegetation and weed removal, and educating others about the natural environment.

Volunteering in Schools

School systems around the world rely heavily on volunteers and donations in order to run effectively. Whenever the economy is down, the need for volunteers and resources increases greatly. There are many opportunities available in the school system for volunteers to take advantage of, especially if you have a special skill or trade. There are not many requirements in order to become a volunteer in the school system. Whether you are a parent, grandparent or just a community member most schools just require a volunteer form be completed. Much like the benefits of any type of volunteerism there are great rewards for the volunteer, student, and school. These benefits include but are not limited to: School Benefits-Provided with additional service without having to have added costs, Teachers are given extra time for educational purposes and planning, A positive relationship between the community and the school. Volunteer Benefits-Parents become involved in their child's school and education, New talents that one never knew they had are discovered, A sense of personal satisfaction, Ability to meet new people and develop new friendships. Student Benefits-Students are given a positive role model, Educational success is encouraged and improved.

Politics

In almost all modern societies, the most basic of all values is people helping people and, in the process, helping themselves. But a tension can arise between volunteerism and the state-provided services, so most countries develop policies and enact legislation to clarify the roles and relationships among stockholders and identify and allocate the necessary legal, social, administrative, and financial support. This is particularly necessary when some voluntary activities are seen as a challenge to the authority of the state, e.g. on 29 January 2001, President Bush cautioned that volunteer groups should supplement, not replace, the work of government agencies. Volunteerism that benefits the state but challenges paid counterparts raises the ire of labour unions representing the paid counterparts as in the case of volunteer fire departments, particularly in combination departments.

Difficulties in this model of volunteering can arise when this is applied across national borders. A state sending volunteers to another state can be viewed as a breach of sovereignty and a lack of respect towards the national government of the proposed recipients. Thus, when states negotiate the offer and acceptance of aid, motivations become important, particularly if donors may postpone assistance or stop it altogether. Three types of conditionality have evolved:

1. Financial accountability: Transparency in the management of funding to ensure that what is done by the volunteers is properly targeted.

2. Policy reform: Requesting governments of developing countries adopt certain social, economic, or environmental policies, the most controversial relating to the privatisation of services traditionally offered by the state.
3. Development objectives: Asking developing countries to adjust specific time-bound economic objectives.

Some international volunteer organisations define their primary mission altruistically as fighting poverty and improving the living standards of people in the developing world, e.g. Voluntary Services Overseas has almost 2,000 skilled professionals working as volunteers to pass on their expertise to local people so that, when they return home, their skills remain. When these organisations work in partnership with governments, the results can be impressive. But when other organisations or individual First World governments support the work of volunteer groups, there can be questions as to whether their real motives are poverty alleviation or wealth creation for some of the poor or policies intended to benefit the donor states. This confusion exists because experience shows that what is volunteered can distort the foreign and economic policy of the country receiving the aid. The economies of many low-income countries suffer from "industrialisation without prosperity" and "investment without growth". This arises because "development assistance" guides many Third World governments to pursue "development" policies that have been wasteful, ill-conceived, unproductive or even so positively destructive that they could not have been sustained without outside support.

Indeed, some of the offers of aid have distorted the general spirit of volunteerism, treating local voluntary action as "contributions in kind", i.e. as conditions requiring local people to earn the right to donor "largesse" by modifying their behaviour. This can be seen as patronising and offensive to the recipients because the aid expressly serves the policy aims of the donors rather than the needs of the recipients. The track record shows that making any aid conditional on policy reforms is often ineffective. Conditionality only works when there is a strong domestic commitment to reform and the recipient governments are democratic, i.e. they are accountable to their own electorates. Volunteer organisations and their funding donors should respect the governments of the countries they wish to help and build on the deep-rooted traditions of people to help one another, and thereby provide an important ingredient for social and democratic development.

In the 1960s Ivan Illich offered an analysis of the role of American volunteers in Mexico in his speech entitled, "To Hell With Good Intentions". His concerns, along with critics such as Paulo Freire and Edward Said, revolve around the notion of altruism as an extension of Christian missionary ideology and the sense of responsibility/obligation driving the concept of noblesse oblige, first developed by the French aristocracy as a moral duty derived from their wealth. Simply stated, these both propose the extension of power and authority over indigenous cultures around the world. Recent critiques of volunteerism come from Westmier and Kahn (1996) and bell hooks (2004). There is also growing concern about the effects of neoliberalism in the field of volunteerism, as witnessed by the increasing influence of corporations on the social programming of non-profit community organisations, particularly through youth work. The field of medical tourism (referring to volunteers travelling overseas to deliver care) has recently attracted negative criticism vis-a-vis the alternative notion of sustainable capacities (working in the context of long-term, locally-run but foreign-supported infrastructures). A preponderance of this criticism has appeared largely in the scientific and peer-reviewed literature. Recently, media outlets with more general readerships have published such criticisms, as well.

Non-Governmental Organisation

Non-governmental organisation (NGO) is a term that has become widely accepted as referring to a legally constituted, non-governmental organisation created by natural or legal persons with no participation or representation of any government. In the cases in which NGOs are funded totally or partially by governments, the NGO maintains its non-governmental status and excludes government representatives from membership in the organisation. Unlike the term *intergovernmental organisation*, "non-governmental organisation" is a term in general use but is not a legal definition. In many jurisdictions these types of organisation are defined as "civil society organisations" or referred to by other names. The number of internationally operating NGOs is estimated at 40,000. National numbers are even higher: Russia has 277,000 NGOs. India is estimated to have between 1 million and 2 million NGOs.

National NGOs go back to antiquity. International non-governmental organisations have a history dating back to at least 1839. Rotary, later Rotary International, was founded in 1905. It has been estimated that by 1914 there were 1083 NGOs. International NGOs were important in the anti-slavery movement and the movement for women's suffrage, and reached a peak at the time of the World Disarmament Conference. The definition of "international NGO" (INGO) is first given in resolution 288 (X) of ECOSOC on February 27, 1950: it is defined as "any international organisation that is not founded by an international treaty". Rapid development of the non-governmental sector occurred in western countries as a result of the processes of restructurisation of the welfare state. Further globalisation of that process occurred after the fall of the communist system and was an important part of the Washington consensus.

Globalisation during the 20th century gave rise to the importance of NGOs. Many problems could not be solved within a nation. International treaties and international organisations such as the World Trade Organisation were perceived as being too centred on the interests of capitalist enterprises. Some argued that in an attempt to counterbalance this trend, NGOs have developed to emphasize humanitarian issues, developmental aid and sustainable development. A prominent example of this is the World Social Forum which is a rival convention to the World Economic Forum held annually in January in Davos, Switzerland. The fifth World Social Forum in Porto Alegre, Brazil, in January 2005 was attended by representatives from more than 1,000 NGOs. Some have argued that in forums like these, NGOs take the place of what should belong to popular movements of the poor.

Others argue that NGOs are often imperialist in nature, that they sometimes operate in a racialised manner in dominant countries, and that they fulfil a similar function to that of the clergy during the high colonial era. The philosopher Peter Hallward argues that they are an aristocratic form of politics. However, this philosophy would suggest that organisations of indigenous peoples are not represented, which is untrue. Whatever the case, NGO transnational networking is now extensive.

Types of NGOs

Apart from "NGO", often alternative terms are used as for example: independent sector, volunteer sector, civil society, grassroots organisations, transnational social movement organisations, private voluntary organisations, self-help organisations and non-state actors (NSA's). Non-governmental organisations are a heterogeneous group. A long list of acronyms has developed around the term "NGO".

These include:

- CSO, short for civil society organisation;
- DONGO: Donor Organised NGO;
- ENGO: short for environmental NGO, such as Global 2000;
- GONGOs are government-operated NGOs, which may have been set up by governments to look like NGOs in order to qualify for outside aid or promote the interests of the government in question;

- INGO stands for international NGO; Oxfam is an international NGO
- QUANGOs are quasi-autonomous non-governmental organisations, such as the International Organisation for Standardisation (ISO). (The ISO is actually not purely an NGO, since its membership is by nation, and each nation is represented by what the ISO Council determines to be the 'most broadly representative' standardisation body of a nation. That body might itself be a non-governmental organisation; for example, the United States is represented in ISO by the American National Standards Institute, which is independent of the federal government. However, other countries can be represented by national governmental agencies; this is the trend in Europe.)
- TANGO: short for technical assistance NGO;
- GSO: Grassroots Support Organisation
- MANGO: short for market advocacy NGO
- CHARDS: Community Health and Rural Development Society.

There are also numerous classifications of NGOs. The typology the World Bank uses divides them into Operational and Advocacy:

The primary purpose of an operational NGO is the design and implementation of development-related projects. One frequently used categorisation is the division into *relief-oriented* versus *development-oriented* organisations; they can also be classified according to whether they stress service delivery or participation; or whether they are religious or secular; and whether they are more public or private-oriented. Operational NGOs can be community-based, national or international. The primary purpose of an Advocacy NGO is to defend or promote a specific cause. As opposed to operational project management, these organisations typically try to raise awareness, acceptance and knowledge by lobbying, press work and activist events. USAID refers to NGOs as *private voluntary organisations*. However many scholars have argued that this definition is highly problematic as many NGOs are in fact state and corporate funded and managed projects with professional staff.

NGOs exist for a variety of reasons, usually to further the political or social goals of their members or funders. Examples include improving the state of the natural environment, encouraging the observance of human rights, improving the welfare of the disadvantaged, or representing a corporate agenda. However, there are a huge number of such organisations and their goals cover a broad range of political and philosophical positions. This can also easily be applied to private schools and athletic organisations.

Methods

NGOs vary in their methods. Some act primarily as lobbyists, while others primarily conduct programmes and activities. For instance, an NGO such as Oxfam, concerned with poverty alleviation, might provide needy people with the equipment and skills to find food and clean drinking water, whereas an NGO like the FFDA helps through investigation and documentation of human rights violations and provides legal assistance to victims of human rights abuses. Others, such as Afghanistan Information Management Services, provide specialised technical products and services to support development activities implemented on the ground by other organisations.

Public Relations

Non-governmental organisations need healthy relationships with the public to meet their goals. Foundations and charities use sophisticated public relations campaigns to raise funds and employ standard lobbying techniques with governments. Interest groups may be of political importance because of their ability to influence social and political outcomes. A code of ethics was established in 2002 by The World Association of Non Governmental NGOs.

Consulting

Project Management

There is an increasing awareness that management techniques are crucial to project success in non-governmental organisations. Generally, non-governmental organisations that are private have either a community or environmental focus. They address varieties of issues such as religion, emergency aid, or humanitarian affairs. They mobilize public support and voluntary contributions for aid; they often have strong links with community groups in developing countries, and they often work in areas where government-to-government aid is not possible. NGOs are accepted as a part of the international relations landscape, and while they influence national and multilateral policy-making, increasingly they are more directly involved in local action.

Staffing

Not all people working for non-governmental organisations are volunteers. The reasons people volunteer are not necessarily purely altruistic, and can provide immediate benefits for themselves as well as those they serve, including skills, experience, and contacts. There is some dispute as to whether expatriates should be sent to developing countries. Frequently this type of personnel is employed to satisfy a donor who wants to see the supported project managed by someone from an industrialised country. However, the expertise these employees or volunteers may have can be counterbalanced by a number of factors: the cost of foreigners is typically higher, they have no grass root connections in the country they are sent to, and local expertise is often undervalued. The NGO sector is an important employer in terms of numbers. For example, by the end of 1995, CONCERN worldwide, an international Northern NGO working against poverty, employed 174 expatriates and just over 5,000 national staff working in ten developing countries in Africa and Asia, and in Haiti.

Funding

Large NGOs may have annual budgets in the hundreds of

millions or billions of dollars. For instance, the budget of the American Association of Retired Persons (AARP) was over US$540 million in 1999. Funding such large budgets demands significant fundraising efforts on the part of most NGOs. Major sources of NGO funding include membership dues, the sale of goods and services, grants from international institutions or national governments, and private donations. Several EU-grants provide funds accessible to NGOs. Even though the term "non-governmental organisation" implies independence from governments, most NGOs depend heavily on governments for their funding. A quarter of the US$162 million income in 1998 of the famine-relief organisation Oxfam was donated by the British government and the EU. The Christian relief and development organisation World Vision collected US$55 million worth of goods in 1998 from the American government. Nobel Prize winner Medecins Sans Frontieres (MSF) (known in the USA as Doctors Without Borders) gets 46% of its income from government sources.

Monitoring and Control

In a March 2000 report on United Nations Reform priorities, former U.N. Secretary General Kofi Annan wrote in favour of international humanitarian intervention, arguing that the international community has a "right to protect" citizens of the world against ethnic cleansing, genocide, and crimes against humanity. On the heels of the report, the Canadian government launched the Responsibility to Protect R2PPDF (434 KiB) project, outlining the issue of humanitarian intervention. While the R2P doctrine has wide applications, among the more controversial has been the Canadian government's use of R2P to justify its intervention and support of the coup in Haiti.

Years after R2P, the World Federalist Movement, an organisation which supports "the creation of democratic global structures accountable to the citizens of the world and call for the division of international authority among separate agencies", has launched Responsibility to Protect-Engaging Civil Society

(R2PCS). A collaboration between the WFM and the Canadian government, this project aims to bring NGOs into lockstep with the principles outlined under the original R2P project. The governments of the countries an NGO works or is registered in may require reporting or other monitoring and oversight. Funders generally require reporting and assessment, such information is not necessarily publicly available. There may also be associations and watchdog organisations that research and publish details on the actions of NGOs working in particular geographic or programme areas. In recent years, many large corporations have increased their corporate social responsibility departments in an attempt to preempt NGO campaigns against certain corporate practices.

As the logic goes, if corporations work *with* NGOs, NGOs will not work *against* corporations. In December 2007, The United States Department of Defence Assistant Secretary of Defence (Health Affairs) S. Ward Casscells established an International Health Division under Force Health Protection & Readiness. Part of International Health's mission is to communicate with NGOs in areas of mutual interest. Department of Defence Directive 3000.05, in 2005, requires DoD to regard stability-enhancing activities as a mission of importance equal to war fighting.

In compliance with international law, DoD has necessarily built a capacity to improve essential services in areas of conflict such as Iraq, where the customary lead agencies (State Department and USAID) find it difficult to operate. Unlike the "co-option" strategy described for corporations, the OASD(HA) recognises the neutrality of health as an essential service. International Health cultivates collaborative relationships with NGOs, albeit at arms-length, recognising their traditional independence, expertise and honest broker status. While the goals of DoD and NGOs may seem incongruent, the DoD's emphasis on stability and security to reduce and prevent conflict suggests, on careful analysis, important mutual interests.

Legal Status

The legal form of NGOs is diverse and depends upon homegrown variations in each country's laws and practices. However, four main family groups of NGOs can be found worldwide:

- Unincorporated and voluntary association
- Trusts, charities and foundations
- Companies not just for profit
- Entities formed or registered under special NGO or non-profit laws.

NGOs are not subjects of international law, as states are. An exception is the International Committee of the Red Cross, which is subject to certain specific matters, mainly relating to the Geneva Convention. The Council of Europe in Strasbourg drafted the European Convention on the Recognition of the Legal Personality of International Non-Governmental Organisations in 1986, which sets a common legal basis for the existence and work of NGOs in Europe. Article 11 of the European Convention on Human Rights protects the right to freedom of association, which is also a fundamental norm for NGOs.

Citizen Organisation

There is a growing movement within the "non"-profit and "non"-government sector to define itself in a more constructive, accurate way. Instead of being defined by "non" words, organisations are suggesting new terminology to describe the sector. The term "civil society organisation" (CSO) has been used by a growing number of organisations, such as the Centre for the Study of Global Governance. The term "citizen sector organisation" (CSO) has also been advocated to describe the sector — as one of citizens, for citizens. This labels and positions the sector as its own entity, without relying on language used for the government or business sectors. However some have argued that this is not particularly helpful given that most NGOs are in fact funded by governments and business and that some NGOs are clearly hostile to independently organised people's organisations.

National Policy on the Voluntary Sector

This Policy is a commitment to encourage, enable and empower an independent, creative and effective voluntary sector, with diversity in form and function, so that it can contribute to the social, cultural and economic advancement of the people of India. The voluntary sector has contributed significantly to finding innovative solutions to poverty, deprivation, discrimination and exclusion, through means such as awareness raising, social mobilisation, service delivery, training, research, and advocacy. The voluntary sector has been serving as an effective non-political link between the people and the Government. This policy recognises the important role that the voluntary sector has to play in various areas and affirms the growing need for collaboration with the voluntary sector by the Government, as well as by the private sector, at the local, provincial and national levels.

Scope of the Policy

In the Policy, voluntary organisations (VOs) mean to include organisations engaged in public service, based on ethical, cultural, social, economic, political, religious, spiritual, philanthropic or scientific & technological considerations. VOs include formal as well as informal groups, such as: community-based organisations (CBOs); non-governmental development organisations (NGDOs); charitable organisations; support organisations; networks or federations of such organisations; as well as professional membership associations. To be covered under the Policy, VOs should broadly have the following characteristics:

a) They are private, *i.e.,* separate from Government
b) They do not return profits generated to their owners or directors
c) They are self-governing, *i.e.,* not controlled by Government

d) They are registered organisations or informal groups, with defined aims and objectives.

Objectives of the Policy

The specific objectives of the policy are listed below:

To create an enabling environment for VOs that stimulates their enterprise and effectiveness, and safeguards their autonomy;

To enable VOs to legitimately mobilize necessary financial resources from India and abroad;

To identify systems by which the Government may work together with VOs, on the basis of the principles of mutual trust and respect, and with shared responsibility; and,

To encourage VOs to adopt transparent and accountable systems of governance and management.

The following paragraphs describe how these objectives are to be achieved.

Establishing an Enabling Environment for the Voluntary Sector

The independence of VOs allows them to explore alternative paradigms of development to challenge social, economic and political forces that may work against public interest and to find new ways to combat poverty, deprivation and other social problems. It is therefore crucial that all laws, policies, rules and regulations relating to VOs categorically safeguard their autonomy, while simultaneously ensuring their accountability. Voluntary organisations may be registered as societies, as charitable trusts, or as non-profit companies under Central or State laws. Some States have adopted the Societies Registration Act (1860), with amendments, while others have independent laws. Similarly, laws relating to charitable trusts vary across States. Over time, many of these laws and their corresponding rules have become complex and restrictive, thus leading to delays, harassment and corruption. As the nodal agency for interface between the Government and the Voluntary Sector, the Planning Commission will encourage State Governments to review prevailing laws & rules and simplify, liberalise and rationalise them as far as possible. In order to facilitate registration of non-profit companies, the Government will examine measures to simplify procedures under section 25 of the Companies Act (1956), including those for license, registration, and remuneration to member-employees.

The Government will also examine the feasibility of enacting a simple and liberal central law that will serve as an alternative all-India statute for registering VOs, particularly those that wish to operate in different parts of the country and even abroad. Such a law would co-exist with prevailing central and state laws, allowing a VO the option of registering under one or more laws, depending on the nature and sphere of its activities. There has been much public debate on the voluntary sector, particularly its governance, accountability, and transparency. It is widely believed that the voluntary sector must address these issues through suitable self-regulation. The Government will encourage the evolution of, and subsequently accord recognition to, an independent, national level, self-regulatory agency for the voluntary sector. At the same time, there is need to bolster public confidence in the voluntary sector by opening it up to greater public scrutiny. The Government will encourage Central and State level agencies to introduce norms for filing basic documents in respect of VOs, which have been receiving funding by Government agencies and placing them in the public domain (with easy access through the internet) in order to inculcate a spirit of public oversight.

Public donation is an important source of funds for the voluntary sector and one that can and must increase substantially. Tax incentives play a positive role in this process. Stocks and shares have become a significant form of wealth in the country today. In order to encourage transfer of shares and stock options to VOs, the Government will consider suitable tax rebates for this form of donation. The Government will also simplify and streamline the system for granting income tax exemption status to charitable projects under the Income Tax Act.

At the same time, the Government will consider tightening administrative and penal procedures to ensure that these incentives are not misused by paper charities for private financial gain. International funding of voluntary organisations plays a small, but significant part in supporting such organisations and their work in the country. An organisation seeking foreign funding must be registered under the Foreign Contribution (Regulation) Act. This law prescribes stringent screening norms that often restrict the ability of VOs to avail foreign funds. When approved, there are problems like funds must be held in a single bank account, thus presenting enormous difficulties to VOs working at different locations. The Government will review the FCRA and simplify its provisions that apply to VOs, from time to time, in consultation with the joint consultative group to be set up by the concerned Ministry (as suggested under para 5.4).

The Central Government has framed guidelines for bilateral agencies to give direct assistance to voluntary organisations for projects of social and economic importance. It controls access to such funds and their utilisation, both through the FCRA and through regulation by the Department of Economic Affairs. This system needs to be simplified in consultation with the joint consultative group to be set up by the concerned Ministry. The Government will encourage all relevant Central and State Government agencies to introduce pre-service and in-service training modules on constructive relations with the voluntary sector. Such agencies should introduce time bound procedures for dealing with the VOs. These would cover registration, income tax clearances, financial assistance, etc. There would be formal systems for registering complaints and for redressing grievances of VOs.

Partnership in Development

The voluntary sector can play an important role in the

development process, particularly through community participation. VOs can offer alternative perspectives; committed expertise; an understanding of the local opportunities and constraints; and perhaps most importantly, the capacity to conduct a meaningful dialogue with communities, particularly those that are disadvantaged. It is therefore essential that the Government and the Voluntary Sector work together. Where feasible, such partnership may also include other entities such as *panchayati raj* institutions, municipalities, academic institutions, and private sector organisations. Partnership between Government and VOs implies identifying shared goals and defining complementary roles. It must be based on the basic principles of mutual trust and respect, with shared responsibility and authority. These principles must be explicit in the terms and conditions of the partnership. They must also be evident in the formal and informal systems of collaboration.

This Policy recognises three instruments of partnership, viz., (i) consultation, through a formal process of interaction at the Centre, State and District level; (ii) strategic collaboration to tackle complex interventions where sustained social mobilisation is critical over the long term; and (iii) project funding through standard schemes. The Government will ensure that these three instruments of partnership are given due attention in Annual Plans prepared by Ministries and States. The action that will be taken in respect of each of the three instruments is discussed in the following paragraphs.

The Government will encourage setting up of Joint Consultative Groups/Forums or Joint Machineries of government and voluntary sector representatives, by relevant Central Departments and State Governments. It will also encourage district administrations, district planning bodies, district rural development agencies, *zilla parishads* and local governments to do so. These groups will be permanent forums with the explicit mandate to share ideas, views and information and to identify opportunities and mechanisms of working together. The Government will introduce suitable mechanisms for involving a wide cross-section of the voluntary sector in these Groups/Forums. The expertise of the voluntary sector will also be utilized, by including experts from VOs in the committees, task forces, and advisory panels constituted by the Government from time to time to help address important issues. The country faces a number of complex problems that require adaptive, multi-sectoral solutions where sustained social mobilisation is particularly important.

These include poverty alleviation, skill promotion, entrepreneurship development, empowerment of women, population stabilisation, combating HIV/AIDS, managing water resources, elementary education and forest management, to name a few. Such areas urgently require strategic collaboration between the Government and VOs, through national level programmes that are long-term in duration, and utilize multiple strategies, methodologies and activities to achieve their objectives. The Government will identify national collaborative programmes to be implemented in partnership with VOs. Each national collaborative programme will involve a finite set of reputed, medium or large VOs with a proven track record, and the ability to work on a reasonably large scale. The Government will ensure that such national collaborative programmes are given due importance in Plan documents.

The third instrument of partnership between the Government and the voluntary sector is project funding. A large number of Government agencies operate schemes for financial assistance to VOs. These schemes usually deal with activities such as surveys, research, workshops, documentation, awareness raising, training, creation and running of public welfare facilities, and so on. Project grants are a useful means for the Government to promote its activities without its direct involvement. They are also a valuable source of support to small and medium VOs. Nevertheless, there are legitimate concerns regarding the effectiveness of grant-in-aid schemes. Out-dated design of funding schemes, arbitrary procedures, selection of unsuitable VOs, poor quality of implementation, and misuse of funds are some of the reasons for the possible defeat of the objectives of such funding. Concerned Government agencies would be encouraged to ensure proper accountability and monitoring of public funds distributed to VOs. Some Central agencies have achieved good results by decentralising the process of project funding. Rather than administering various schemes directly, they appoint regional or State level intermediary organisations to do so on their behalf. This allows for closer interaction for better selection and monitoring of VOs. Intermediaries could include umbrella VOs, professional or academic institutes, State Government agencies, or multi-stockholder standing committees.

The Government will review the experience of such decentralised funding and make suitable recommendations to Central agencies. There is reason to believe that accreditation of VOs will lead to better funding decisions and make the funding processes more transparent. Further, accreditation may provide incentives for better governance, management and performance of VOs. No reliable accreditation system is in place at present. The Government will encourage various agencies, including those in the voluntary sector, to develop alternative accreditation methodologies. It will allow time for such methodologies to be debated and gain acceptability in the voluntary sector, before considering their application to Government funding of VOs.

Strengthening the Voluntary Sector

The Indian society has a well-established tradition of philanthropy. While a regime of tax concessions facilitates donations to charitable organisations, there is considerable untapped potential to channelise private wealth for public service. The Government will support and encourage existing, as well new, independent philanthropic institutions and private foundations to provide financial assistance to deserving VOs. It will also promote a dialogue among public and private grant makers so that they may take advantage of the best practices in grant making and fund-raising strategies. Accountability to all stockholders and transparency in functioning are key issues in good governance. The voluntary sector is expected to set its own benchmarks in these areas. Since VOs vary in their objectives and activities, it would be impractical to expect uniform norms for accountability and transparency. The Government will encourage support organisations, and VO networks & federations to facilitate discussion and consensus building on these issues. It will also encourage such agencies to advise and assist VOs to adopt norms that they find acceptable and useful.

The Government will recognise excellence in governance among VOs by publicising best practices. Training is a crucial requirement for people working in the voluntary sector. However, this is often neglected on account of limited availability of good quality training courses that are reasonably priced. The Government will support and encourage organisations that train aspirants to enter the voluntary sector, as well as those already working in the sector. It will make available physical facilities currently available with its training institutes as a measure of such support. Innovation in institutional, technical and social approaches to development problems is an essential ingredient of voluntary action. The Government will encourage and recognise innovative & pioneering work.

Databases of VOs working in different fields and at different levels are useful for communication within the voluntary sector, as well as between the voluntary sector and the public & private sector. The Government will commission suitable agencies to prepare and update such databases. Information on Government policies and programmes is often difficult for VOs to access. The websites of various Government agencies will be re-designed to provide links to key documents and databases, including those related to project funding schemes. The Government will encourage involvement of volunteers in public services, such as, at family welfare centres, primary health centres, hospitals, schools, vocational training centres, sanitation campaigns, etc. This National Policy on the Voluntary Sector-2007 is the beginning of a process to evolve a new working relationship between the Government and the Voluntary Sector, without affecting the autonomy and identity of VOs.

REFERENCES

Campbell, Donald, 1971, "Methods for Experimenting Society: (Paper presented at the meeting of the American Psychological Association, Washington, D.C.: September.

Cicarelli, Victor, *ed al,* 1969, *The Impact of Head Start,* Springfield, Virgirica: U.S. Clearing House for Federal Scientific and Technical Information.

Dunn, William, 1986, *Policy Analysis: Perspectives, Concepts and Methods,* Greenwich, Ct: J.A.I Press.

Durkneim, Emile, 1958, *Socialism and Saint-Simon* (Le Socialisme) ed. by Alvin W. Gouldner, Ohio: Yellow Springs.

Lowry, Richie P., 1974, *Social Problems:* A Critical Analysis of Theories and Public Policy, Lexington, Mass.: D.C. Heath.

MacRae, Duncan, and James Wilde, *1979, Policy Analysis for Public* Decisions, N. Scituate, Ma.: Duxbury.

CHAPTER 3

Contemporary Social Welfare Systems and Civil Society

> I've a problem with the word charity because I think that NGOs, as I prefer calling them, really do take the work of moral and social responsibilities that ought to be taken on by governments.
>
> —*Emma Thompson*

Analysing the Development of Contemporary Social Welfare Systems

Each of the three conventional approaches to studying the development of contemporary social welfare systems—the political economy approach, the moral economy approach and the mixed economic approach—is based on a distinctive analytical model, each with its own conceptual frameworks, theoretical preferences, and normative commitments. While each approach has contributed significantly to our understanding of how and why social welfare systems develop, disciplinary boundaries and distinctive research agendas have tended to thwart cross fertilisation among them.

Thus, looking more closely at how they compare to one another is important not only for identifying the social economy perspective as an emergent alternative, but also for generating a more integrated, informed understanding of the impact of globalisation on social development in the twenty-first century.

The Political Economy Approach

Emerging during a period of profound faith in the state as the key to prosperity and progress, the political economy approach reflects the social ideals of the post-war era: universalism, equality, and the power of the state to provide an unprecedented quality of life for its citizens. The welfare state, its key unit of analysis, is conceptualised as a form of embedded liberalism—a reformist compromise capable of compensating for, if not correcting, the most deleterious affects of the capitalist economy. Although initially focused on the political engineering of social protection vis-a-vis social rights and regulations, with the end of the so-called Golden Age of the welfare state, the political economy approach has focused on questions and issues pertaining to welfare retrenchment and the respective role of politics and economics in driving welfare reform. Although long a concern within liberal welfare states like the United States, more recent debates about an emerging global "third way" (Giddens, 2001) and the transformation of "vice into virtue" among conservative, christian democratic welfare states have drawn attention to the ways in which welfare states are 'recalibrating' and the relevant degree of freedom they have in dealing effectively with the cultural and economic challenges of globalisation. Within the political economy framework, the key point of contention focuses on the extent to which there has been greater convergence or persistent divergence among historically distinctive models of welfare state development.

The convergence thesis holds that welfare states, particularly those characterised by comprehensive, national social programmes and public services, face growing external constraints to their ability to maintain generous, publicly financed social protections. According to this thesis, shifting patterns in international trade and finance increase competitive pressures within the global economy, thus restricting government's maneuverability in crafting policy to meet domestic social and economic objectives. As traditional macro-economic policy tools become harder to manage and labour and total production costs rise due to the diversification of demand and the increasing use of technology, governments must rely heavily on non-payroll taxes to finance welfare expenditures.

Yet high rates of inflation combined with shrinking tax bases make substantial tax increases both economically and politically unpopular. Combined with significant pressures to reduce budget deficits, this situation places critical limits to the expansion of social spending and thus the ability and willingness of governments to provide wide-ranging, long term public benefits. In addition to scaling back cash-based subsidies and increasing eligibility requirements, devolving competencies to lower levels of government and off-loading services to private providers are seen as the logical product of welfare states' increasing vulnerability to the vagaries of market forces. The divergence thesis, by contrast, is advanced by those who see the link between economic imperatives and policy choices as over determined. From this perspective, political preferences, policy legacies, and institutional arrangements are conditioned by historically driven, path-dependent processes which mitigate if not compel differential responses to common challenges. Because powerful structural, political and cultural forces are seen as mediating both policy makers perception of the challenges arising from globalisation as well as their responses to them, different types of welfare states are seen as posing unique constraints and opportunities for reform. And because social reform reflects tensions generated by existing sociopolitical cleavages, cultural values, and strategic maneuvering by relevant political actors, the divergence thesis expects that reform will reflect the adoption of a wide range of policy tools.

hus, while decentralisation and privatisation may be standard policy proposals across a variety of welfare states, the specific policies formulated and implemented will vary. Thus, whereas the introduction of new technology systems aimed at maximising choice and increasing economic efficiency is expected in Liberal welfare states like the United States and Great Britain, it is less likely in continental European countries where the legacies of familialism and paternalism are stronger and budget control is a higher priority.

While the political economy approach to welfare reform offers an important contribution to our understanding of the constraints and opportunities facing governments as they attempt to craft solutions to the challenges raised by globalisation, one of its key drawbacks is that by emphasising convergence vs. divergence, it is of limited utility in helping us to better understand the more nuanced dynamics of welfare reform. While the state is imbued with responsibility and control over welfare, society is seen primarily as the passive recipient of state-generated policies and prescriptions. Thus, arguments about the positive or negative effect of reforms on social welfare tend to be based almost exclusively on their implications for the state. Either they are increasing the state's capacity to effectively and fairly respond to social needs or undermining its efforts to maintain its commitments to reasonable, equitable and/or just social benefits. A second, yet related problem with the political economy approach is that in focusing on the nation-state as its primary, and in most cases exclusive, level of analysis, the space between policy making and policy outcomes remains a black box. In confining the analysis of globalisation and its subsequent affects on welfare reform to "high politics," understood as elite-level policy formation, the political economy approach underestimates or leaves out important dynamics that operate in the realm of "low politics," as well as a variety of cross cutting territorial and sector-based considerations that profoundly impact the inter-play between policy making and policy implementation and thus the substantive impact that welfare reform has on users and citizens.

The Moral Economy Approach

Whereas the political economy approach is fuelled by a profound skepticism about the ability of society to meet the collective social needs of citizens, the moral economy approach embraces community as the primary guardian of social well being. Grounded in a conception of welfare provision as the natural extension of voluntary, mutualistic forms of self-help, the moral economy approach offers an alternative framework for conceptualising and analysing social welfare systems as a product of the so-called welfare society, a model for organising social welfare on the basis of interlocking individual sanctions and rewards emanating from local communities. The moral economy approach can be further separated into a progressive and a conservative version based on distinctive interpretations of the social fabric of society. The conservative version of the welfare society is profoundly skeptical of the governments' ability to gauge social needs and harness capitalism to fulfil these needs.

Emerging as a reaction to the state's perceived colonisation of civil society, this version of the moral economy perspective underscores the dangers of publicly provided, state-regulated welfare. Conceptualised as a paternalistic bureaucracy, the state is seen as creating harmful 'welfare dependencies,' which erode personal responsibility and weaken the ability of people to help themselves by undermining community-based social and ethnical norms. By contrast, the welfare society, which is viewed as complementing, rather than competing with market-based exchange mechanisms, is seen as strengthening the social fabric of society by reinforcing traditional values such as family loyalty and social obligation.

A more progressive version of the moral economy approach embraces the welfare society not as the locus of cultural preservation, but rather as part of a broader movement toward social solidarity and associative democracy. Emphasising participation and connectedness to local community as a principle legitimating factor in empowering and assisting people in need, this perspective sees reciprocity as a necessary precursor to developing healthy and productive societies. Less a reaction to the state than a response to the commerciahsation and alienation that has accompanied the process of modernisation, this version of the moral economy approach sees communities as critical to actively reconstituting society by reconstructing identities and extending affective bonds between groups of people that increasingly lack a shared moral culture.

From this perspective, the welfare society embodies a realm of fluid, multi-faceted relationships which counteract individualism and narrow self interest by fostering trust, mutual respect, and collective participation. Regardless of their distinctive under standings of the social fabric of the welfare society, both versions of the moral economy approach underscore the importance of social actors, emotive ideas, and the non-rationality of culture in the development of social welfare systems. Challenging the authority of the state as legitimate arbitrator of welfare reform, they expand the scope of inquiry beyond the political economy approach's relatively narrow focus on poverty rates, social security, and income-transfers to encompass a broader array of social arrangements and processes, from more traditional conceptions of self-help to community care and the creation of alternative consciousness.

Despite this noteworthy advantage, the moral economy approach suffers from several shortcomings. First, by ignoring, by and large, the distributional aspects of social welfare systems, it obscures the important role that societal stratification and inequality play in welfare reform. Because the most marginalised segments of the population usually lack the capacity to voice their concerns and press their needs effectively, they tend to be disadvantaged by a welfare society which relies predominately if not exclusively on self identification of need and voluntary responses to those needs. Second, the moral economy approach reproduces the state-society dualism of the political economy approach, thus obscuring rather than clarifying the relationship between the two realms.

By viewing he welfare society as an autonomous locus of proactive community engagement, responsive to both individual want and collective need, the moral economy approach portrays the state as outside of, and thus largely irrelevant to, society. Where the state is considered, however, the focus of the moral economy approach is almost exclusively on its coercive power. As a result, it tends to underestimate the state's role in establishing the foundation for effective responses to a variety of welfare dilemmas, including stimulating the welfare enhancing properties of community activism by, for example, outlawing discriminatory practices, redistributing scarce resources, and guaranteeing social rights. A third problem with the moral economy approach is that it does not pay adequate attention to the multiplicity of institutional configurations involved in the day-to-day operation of social welfare systems. Consequently, it fails to appreciate the extent to which the distinctive juridical and legal status of private and non-profit organisations is critical to the success of welfare reform.

The Mixed Economy Approach

The growing complexity of the inter-organisational linkages connecting social organisations to one another and to public institutions, and the recognition of this development as critical to determining the consequences of welfare reform, has led to the development of a third approach, frequently defined as the mixed economy of welfare. While those who employ this approach come from a wide array of disciplines, principally economics, but also social welfare, public administration, and non-profit management, they ground their analysis in a concept of the welfare mix which is distinctive from both that of the welfare society the welfare state. The concept of the welfare mix emphasizes institutional plurality and shared responsibility for welfare.

Inevitably, social welfare systems draw on a variety of organisational resources, all of which are embedded within a broader set of exchange and production relationships. As the guarantor of citizen's legal entitlements and a key source of power, the state, understood more broadly as the public sector, is recognised as playing a vital role in the creation of social markets, understood as quasi-markets for social goods and services which separate purchasers, usually government agencies, from providers. The public sector is balanced, however, by two equally important sectors, the private and non-profit sectors, each of which operates according to a unique set of norms and principles.

Thus, within the mixed economy approach, it is the relationship between the public, private and non-profit sectors that determines temporal and spatial variation in the output of social welfare systems. Emphasising institutional plurality, the mixed economy approach to welfare offers an analytic framework in which the output of welfare systems varies both temporally and spatially according to the relationship between the public, private and non-profit sectors.

Thus, in addition to identifying a third sector, distinct from both the state and society, the mixed economy approach has contributed to our understanding of social welfare systems by paving the way for more sophisticated longitudinal and comparative empirical analysis of welfare systems across a variety of local and national contexts. While paving the way for a more sophisticated comparative analysis of welfare systems and their capacity to mediate pressures for reform, the mixed economy approach has two significant limitations. First, by assuming a difference in kind between organisations according to the presence or absence of certain sector-based properties and functions, the welfare mix approach falls into the same dilemma of the previous two approaches.

It fails to fully appreciate the breadth and depth of organisational variation within each sector, thus divorcing pertinent issues relating to social production (i.e. contracting, management, participation) from core issues of policy reform (i.e. cost effectiveness, marginalisation, entitlement issues). Second, in focusing on the technical and economic aspects of institutional performance, it obscures the social and political relevance of reform.

By failing to link institutional outputs to the types of system-wide properties that give them meaning for those that they affect most directly, such as marginalised citizens and welfare users, the mixed economy approach does little to improve our understanding of the issues related to social justice.

An Emerging Paradigm: The Social Economy Approach to Welfare Reform

More recently, a growing body of work emerging from the social economy literature has established the basis for a new approach to welfare reform. Motivated by a shared set of theoretical and empirical concerns about the role of the third sector in mediating the relationship between state, society, and economy, this social economy approach is distinct from conventional approaches in that it offers an alternative conceptual understanding of social welfare systems as dynamic, open systems, grounded in complex institutional networks.

In addition, it seeks to accumulate knowledge about collective forms of entrepreneurship and the extent to which they act as catalysts of change within emerging welfare networks. Like political economy and moral economy approaches, the social economy approach is concerned about macro-level developments in the economy and society. Yet, it links these changes to questions and concerns relating to the social and administrative underpinnings of social welfare. As such, it introduces greater dynamism by exploring the micro foundations of institutional change, thus avoiding the political and moral economy approaches' over-emphasis on the degree to which macro-level structural and cultural forces Favour continuity over change within social welfare systems.

Although recognising that third sector organisations may rarely determine social and economic outcomes on their own, the social economy approach underscores their critical role in establishing the context and meaning that determine how every day people perceive of and experience social welfare. While overlapping with the mixed economy approach in its attention to the third sector, the social economy approach encompasses a broader understanding of the third sector as a highly differentiated and interpenetrated institutional realm neither derivative of, nor inherently in competition with, the public and private sectors. In proposing a more fluid conceptualisation of the third sector as an important nexus of interaction between different principles (i.e. exchange, redistribution, and reciprocity) otherwise seen as distinctive characteristics of either economy, state, or community, the social economy approach moves beyond conventional under standings of market values and interests and social values and interests as inherently conflicting.

Embedded in both society and the economy, third sector organisations create, reconstruct and maintain social relationships as well as the universe of practices and forms of mobilising economic resources, which, as Saucier and Thivierge (2003) observe, are key to combating poverty, generating social solidarity, and satisfying human needs.

The Rise of Welfare Networks

The social economy approach takes for granted that the processes of globalisation and modernisation have fundamentally altered the parameters of contemporary welfare systems, and thus its principle concern is in understanding the capacity of third sector organisations to serve as a socially efficacious response to these twin challenges. Although identifying and explaining the causes of broader structural change is not a central component of the social economy approach, its analysis of the third sector's role in responding to change is informed by an understanding of globalisation and modernisation as symptomatic of a fundamental shift in the productive infrastructure of society from one which was industrial to one which is predominately informational and service based. By impacting employment opportunities and family dynamics, this structural shift in the economy significantly impacts the demographic composition of society, which in turn fuels greater pressures toward administrative, political and economic decentralisation.

While these processes significantly increase the complexity of welfare systems, the capacity of national public administrators to manage social welfare systems diminishes as greater policy responsibility is transferred to the subnational level, shifting the locus of public intervention away from the central government to lower levels of government. In tandem with a pervasive post-materialist shift in values post-in-dustrialism entails a transition away from both the state and society as dominant organising infrastructures of the social welfare systems toward more amorphous welfare networks. This reconstitution of welfare systems into welfare networks motivates three key developments:

1) The potential for constructing more efficacious responses to new and old social and economic risks, and
2) The emergence of a more complex and differentiated third sector, and
3) A more fluid process of reform facilitated by the proliferation of new organisational forms and strategies utilised in social welfare provision.

Social Risk and Emerging Welfare Networks

The key characteristics defining the new post-industrial era—the blurring of boundaries between sectors, the increasing specialisation and volatility of social and economic relations, and the institutionalisation of continual change—both exacerbate pre-existing risks and create new ones. They restrict the relevant degree of freedom afforded to governments to adopt and implement social policies that can harness the benefits and compensate for the losses incurred by globalisation and modernisation, thus contributing to what Beck (1998) identifies as the 'democratisation of vulnerability' as risk becomes more fluid.

Greater instability and increasing differentiation in citizens' needs and preferences make it increasingly difficult for public officials to guarantee a fair and equitable allocation of social and economic resources and a high standard of living to all citizens while the combination of diminishing public resources, increasing ethnic and cultural diversity (and with it the proliferation of social customs, norms, and practices) increase the threat of various forms of discrimination. In tandem with these developments, welfare networks offer the potential for constructing more efficacious responses to risk, particularly those related to social exclusion and economic dependency.

In much the same way that the creation of the market economy during the nineteenth century gave rise to what economic historian Karl Polanyi (1944) describes as a double movement, the social and economic processes set in motion by the current post-industrial shift has engendered a countermovement. This countermovement, stimulated by the impulse to re-embed the economy in social relations, creates a new role for third sector organisations as the source of alternative social constructions capable of generating a collective response to social need.

Although not intrinsically a promoter of social justice, in a context in which globalisation, combined with a maturation of government commitments increases citizens' vulnerability to social dislocation while simultaneously undermining the capacity and legitimacy of the state to provide social protection, the third sector represents a force within local communities that works to make them more livable, and in many ways, more socially just.

By creating new forms of connectivity and solidarity, covering new forms of social need, and mobilising citizen awareness of and reaction to factors which undermine the public good, third sector organisations alleviate social marginalisation, negotiate greater fairness.

The Civil Society in the Welfare State

This report on the civil society in the Swedish welfare state is based on 2,749 telephone interviews conducted with a random sample from the population register of persons 16-89 years of age throughout Sweden. The interviews were conducted in the Spring of 1994, at the bottom of a deep recession. The fieldwork was carried out by Demoskop AB from its telephone interviewing facilities in Stockholm. The analysis was done at Value Scope AB in Stockholm.

The Civil Society

In Sweden, with its focus on state-run welfare, the role of the civil society has long been ignored in public and political discourse. We find, however, that it not only is flourishing but also constitutes an essential part of the social fabric and represents the most meaningful aspect of life for the citizens of the Swedish welfare state.

The civil society includes family life, neighbourhood and community life, social activities, activities in voluntary associations, and religious and cultural activities. Our focus on the role of the civil society in welfare questions indicates that we need to complement the political scientist's view of Swedish civil society by bringing in family and community life.

FamilyLife

The general discourse in the media can convey the impression that the end of the 1910s finds the Swedish family weak and fairly insignificant. A review of our statistical data provides a different picture, one of stronger family bonds and responsibilities. The representation of a weak family in the general discourse is true of a minority, not of the majority. In the 1910s most adults continue to live with others (77%) and thereby have daily contact with the most prevalent form of community life in the civil society.

Single parents are not common: 6 percent of all women aged 16-44 years are mothers with children 14 years of age or younger who live without a spouse or partner; the figure for fathers who live alone with minor children is 0.4 percent. In older age groups it is usual that one's children have moved from the parental home and that one has grandchildren. Among persons under 64 years of age, almost all have parents or parents-in-law who are living. Practically all individuals who live in Sweden thus have some close relative. The nuclear family has changed significantly during recent generations. A half century ago, when a person moved from his parental home, both parents were usually still living in the home; if one of them was not in the home it was because he or she was deceased. Even today's youth usually have both parents living at home when he or she moves; only one out of five young people say that one parent had moved before he or she did so.

Although the divorce rate has risen, three out of four young people have *not* experienced divorce or death among their parents. The idea that today's family is in dissolution and has ceased to function is thus not true for a majority of young people. The civil society also comprises social life and activities in voluntary associations. With few exceptions, all those interviewed mix at least some of the time with both relatives and friends. Our interview dealt among other things with the family, work, helpfulness, and subsidies from the welfare state. At the end of the 30-minute long interview, the respondent was asked: "When you look back, what has given you the most in life? Is it your work, family life, social life, participation in voluntary associations, or your life as a citizen in a welfare state?"

When it comes down to it, it is family life, social life, and participation in voluntary associations-that is, the civil society-which most people have experienced as most meaningful. Of all those interviewed, 60 percent were of this opinion. Every fourth person (28%) reported that work had been the most meaningful area in their life. Every tenth person (10%) answered that life as a citizen in a welfare state had been most meaningful to them. The media and the public discourse are filled with discussions about the problems of the economy and working life and with the problems of the welfare state. However, life in the civil society is most meaningful to the man on the street. Of all adults 16-89 years of age in 1994, 84 percent live on income from the labour market in the form of employment, extra jobs, or pensions from previous employment.

By comparison, the proportion with income derived from the civil society is low-31 percent. One out of 20 persons receives cash contributions from family and relatives. As many have received some inheritance. Every fourth person has his own savings, income from capital or property, the sale of stocks or other assets. Routinely distributed benefits from the state which the recipient need not apply for are provided to 43 percent of the population.

Old-age pensions and child allowances constitute the largest share of such benefits. Of the total population, 28 percent live entirely or partly on benefits that the recipients must apply for, such as housing allowances, student allowances, unemployment compensation, and disability pensions. One and the same person can receive income from different sources and our figures represent percentages of people, not percentages of income in crowns.

The transition of industrial society to a non-industrial society-an information society with a great deal of knowledge imbedded in products and services-is changing the salaried form of work that was the cornerstone of social structure in the 1900s. The old view of salaried work as durable full-time employment with normal working hours for a stable employer is now disintegrating into an increasingly fragmented reality. We will discuss six ways of acquiring a livelihood in Sweden today: Two-thirds of the general public 16-89 years of age are gainfully employed:

- 28 percent are employed in the public sector
- 26 percent are employed in the private sector
- 8 percent are self-employed
- 4 percent work "on a free basis".

One-third of the Swedes 16-89 years of age are not gainfully employed:

- 14.5 percent are 64 years of age or younger (looking for work, 7%, students, 3%, early or partial retirees, 3%, other, 2%)
- 20 percent are 65 years of age or older.

The very high number employed in public service is a

reflection of the extensive nature of the Swedish welfare state in which the government not only finances welfare programmes but also runs them as public bureaucracies. Our classification is conventional, with the exception of the category "work on a free basis," an answer that was given by one out of 25 people. They do not consider themselves to be employed or to be self-employed.

We have here a modern category of free-lancers. They are "engaged" rather than "employed." One can read data about well-known phenomena such as employment and the length and disposition of working hours from the point of view of the civil society rather than from that of economics. We can then see how much is left over for the civil society once gainful employment has taken its share.

Work Hours

Involvement in the civil society on the part of the gainfully employed is limited by the length of their working hours. The combination of a high degree of employment and a large proportion of people with normal working hours restrains the activities of the civil society, This means that the lion's share of those gainfully employed are pulled out of the civil society at the same hours of the day and away from activities such as child care and care of the aged. In Sweden the dilemma has been resolved by moving much of the care of children and of the aged to public institutions. What has not been fully recognised is that the dilemma has also been resolved by departing from the usual work week and work hours.

Gainful employment is not limited to daytime hours Monday to Friday. It is true that 73 percent of those gainfully employed state that they work "normal working hours, that is Monday through Friday, sometime between 7 am and 6 pm", but four out of ten work on weekends or nights or late in the evening, and every fourth works early morning hours. There is a stunning contrast between our findings and that which legislators, union negotiators, social planners and others assume to be normal and universally applicable-namely, full-time employment between 8 and 5, Monday through Friday. When we examined the percentage of people who work only "normal" work hours (which, in our question, were extended to between 7 am and 6 pm) Monday through Friday, and who have a normal work week of 35 or 40 hours, we found that only every fourth person with gainful employment (27%) fitted this category (27% of blue collar workers, 37 percent of white collar workers and 7% of the self-employed). Despite the many arrangements of work hours, the full need for flexibility has not been fulfilled.

Every other person with normal work hours and preschool children wants to change his/her work hours in order to spend more time during the day with the children. There is a conservatism in the view of work hours entertained by the authorities, the unions, and parliament. The Swedish civil society struggles successfully for its existence against these powers in regard to the question of work hours.

Job Hunters and the Unemployed

The interviews contain questions about occupation and about how one acquires a livelihood. In answer to the question about occupation, 9 percent (183 persons) between the ages of 16 and 64 said that they lack gainful employment but are looking for work; they are below retirement age and state that they have no gainful employment, no work from which they have sick leave or other forms of leave, and no other paid work. In answer to the question about how one gains a livelihood, 7 percent (136 persons) stated that they receive unemployment compensation or labour market assistance.

These categories-the jobless and those who receive unemployment compensation-overlap only partially. Of the 136 persons interviewed who receive unemployment compensation, about one-half (55%) said that they were job hunting. According to their own statements given in our interviews, the other half (45%) are not looking for work. We find that 3 percent of the population between the ages of 16 and 64 practice that which sociologists term "institutionalised evasion of institutional rules". Those who receive unemployment compensation are obliged to look for work, but not all do so.

The unions and the authorities evidently look the other way. The old, formally accepted rules are stretc..hed to accomodate them to new, informally accepted norms. Of those who have received unemployment compensation, 36 percent had some paid work the days just preceding the interview. Here we can detect yet another example of the bending of rules. Job hunters and the unemployed have several different sources of income. Students' assistance, which in Sweden is part subsidy and part loan, is the most usual income source for those without a job who are looking for work but do not receive unemployment compensation.

Job hunters who receive unemployment compensation get along mainly on that income. The third category receives unemployment compensation at the same time as s/he has a job; in addition, some receive welfare and housing allowances and/or financial help from parents or other relatives. On the whole, Sweden's social safety net managed to do its job during 1994, a year of deep recession and record high unemployment. This was not only the result of Sweden's special labour market policies. It was also due to that fact that almost all the unemployed are involved in a number of contexts in the private, public, and civil sectors which provide them with means of subsistence. In addition, in some cases the official rules for granting benefits have been reinterpreted to follow a new, informal praxis.

Several Sources of Income

The chapter concludes with a review of the income sources in the different population segments. One-third of the self-employed (34%) receive automatic state benefits, usually child allowances, as a supplement to their income from their own business. Those who work on a free basis do not support themselves solely from such work; all of 48 percent also applied for benefits, usually in the form of student assistance, advance payments on maintenance allowances for children, child support, and housing allowances. Every sixth person who was employed in the private sector also moonlighted (16%); 26 percent received child allowances and 6 percent received housing allowances.

The income sources of those employed in the public sector resembled those of people employed in the private sector: 16 percent moonlighted, 32 percent received child allowances, and 6 percent received housing allowances. Those without gainful employment of some kind who were below retirement age lived mainly on state benefits for which one must apply: student assistance (36%), disability pensions (22%), unemployment compensation, (23%), housing allowances (15%). Many-more than any other group-also receive income from the civil society, primarily in the form of assistance from family and/or relatives (19%). Many old-age pensioners who were not gainfully employed had their own savings with which to supplement other income sources (39%). This group also had the highest incidence of recipients of housing allowances (16%). One must be careful with claims such as x percent live on the market economy, y percent live off relatives, and z percent live off the state.

Most people have more than one source of income, and this applies to all segments in society. In all of Sweden, for example, only 16 percent of people between the ages of 16 and 89 have neither a job in the public sector nor receive any benefits or pensions from it. Furthermore, the odds are small that these 16 percent do not have a wife/husband, parents or children who receive some form of payments from the public sector.

Private Transfers

Togetherness, personal contacts, and the ideal of helping one another characterize the civil society. In our research, these features were illuminated in questions asking how children and parents help one another, and how people generally offer time, goods, and money to assist others. Public discourse about welfare in Sweden has seldom paid attention to such transfers; it has instead been predicated on the assumption that all transfers are achieved through political decisions. "Transfers" is a term used in the state bureaucracy; we did not use it in our interviews. The term is not to be found in the vocabulary of the civil society.

Here one speaks of gifts and services and reciprocity, of consideration, love, help, and solicitude. This theme has many variations, and we can present here only a few examples, not the whole picture. Of all those interviewed, 79 percent reported that they have provided or received assistance in kind in one or more of the ways which we exemplified in our survey, namely, by receiving house guests or being afforded such hospitality, or by showing generosity to relatives and friends by giving away garden products, a catch of fish or game. Altogether 81 percent have given financial assistance to children, parents, parents-in-law, husband, wife, or partner, or have made donations to charitable organisations.

Many help children and grandchildren financially. Every third parent with children who have moved from the parental home has at some time vouched for their bank loans. A considerable portion of leisure time is spent caring for and helping others. Children help their parents, and many people have relatives who are sick, handicapped, or old and who require care and attention. A total of 84 percent help others by contributing their time or efforts. Younger people help others significantly more by contributing their time, while older people help others significantly more through financial contributions. Interestingly enough, work hours do not have much bearing on how one helps others. It is true that people with short work hours have more time to devote to gardening, fishing, and hunting, and can contribute material goods more than those with long work hours, while they also have fewer resources to help others financially.

Yet people with long work hours also devote a great deal of time-more than the average-to assisting those close to them. In smaller communities and on the countryside is above the average for help in the form of material goods. However, the degree of urbanisation of residential area does not affect the extent to which assistance is rendered in terms of time or money.

Those who own their own business-often a small family firm-constitute a group with a high degree of social responsibility. They represent the highest percentages of assistance rendered in respect to both caring activities and private transfers. They have one foot in the civil society, the other in the marketplace. People with the lowest household incomes are naturally less able to help others financially. However, the index for them lies under the average even in respect to assistance rendered in time or in material goods. Many older people belong to this income group.

A review of private transfers in Sweden shows that they are prodigious. I shall not attempt to translate their value into crowns. Any attempt at such a translation on the basis of the available data would require too many arbitrary assumptions. It should be noted, however, that it will be difficult to present these transfers as a percentage of the GNP since most of them do not enter into the basis for calculating the GNP. An objection to the thought of calculating the transfers of the civil society is the idea that gifts, services, and reciprocal acts belong to a category that should not carry a price tag, according to the ethos of the civil society. But everyone, even an economist, removes the price tag before s/he gives away a gift.

The behaviour of researchers follows other rules that those of private individuals, and we consider that such calculations represent a legitimate project for future research. The simple conclusion that I wish to emphasize is that welfare in Sweden is by no means synonymous with welfare under public auspices. The network of mutual assistance of the civil society can be found in all segments of society. Other questions for future research could concern the interpretation of the renown success of Swedish welfare.

To what extent do the private activities of the civil society actually constitute a silent and hidden prerequisite for public welfare undertakings? To what extent are private transfers dependent on the existence of a base of public transfers? And-the most important research project-has Swedish welfare legislation been in harmony with the transfers of the civil society or has it staunched the flow of generosity of the civil society?

Caring in The Civil Society

It has been said that care giving functions in Sweden are socialized, that is, they are administered and carried out by the public sector. But many private individuals care for someone who is sick, handicapped, or elderly. In this chapter we wish to draw attention to such informal caring as a central function in the civil society. One of the fundamental norms of the civil society holds that we must not fail those close to us when they are in need. International research on caring discusses both *nursing* and *caring*. Our concern here is with caring, not with nursing. Slightly more than every fifth adult 16-89 years of age (22%) is a care in the civil society: five percent of all adults in Sweden look after a member of the household who is sick, handicapped, or elderly, and 18 percent regularly tend to someone who does not live in the household; one percent tend to someone in the household as well as to someone who does not share the same domicile.

This totals to approximately 1,6 million individuals who are careers. The Swedish percentage of the population who are careers is slightly higher than the corresponding figure in the United Kingdom; some years ago that figure was 15 percent: four percent tended to someone in the same household and 12 percent tended to someone who did not live in the same household. Many perhaps envisage careers as middle-aged women, but our results show that both men and women and persons of all ages are careers in the civil society: 23 percent of the women and 20 percent of the men in Sweden look after someone in or outside of their households. There is hardly any difference in respect to caring between those who are gainfully employed and those who are not.

Of all those gainfully employed, every fourth individual (23%) looks after or helps someone who is sick, handicapped or elderly; the corresponding figure for those not gainfully employed is 21 percent, and for pensioners, 20 percent. In some cases municipalities provide caretaking that runs parallel to that provided by the civil society. Some of this is in the form of financial support to relatives who act as careers, and some in the form of public domestic assistance. As we saw, 22 percent of all adults in Sweden are careers.

Of these, 8 percent assume their tasks with some financial support from public treasuries, but 14 percent do so without any public financial support. These figures indicate that there are approximately 450,000 men and 560,000 women who are careers without receiving any assistance from municipalities either in the form of public domestic assistance to the care recipient or payments to the care. In the 2,749 interviews carried out, we found 601 persons who look after someone at home or in another household. Careers in the civil society primarily tend to family members (77%). Every third care in the home looks after a husband or wife, every fourth looks after children, and as many tend to parents or parents-in-law. The picture is different for those who tend to someone who does not live in the same household: 37 percent look after parents or parents-in-law, and 28 percent help some other relative, 21 percent of careers help a friend or neighbour, 9 percent help an acquaintance, and 5 percent help someone with whom they have come in contact through an association, church, or the like. Some of the care ministered in the home is quite demanding physically. Many careers assist others by lifting them and physically supporting them in, for example, getting in and out of bed and walking, and help them with their personal hygiene. Their duties may include responsibility for administering medication, injections, and for bandaging, and may thus border on nursing. Careers who look after others outside of the home rarely have duties of this kind.

Most careers, both within and outside of the home, help with practical tasks such as shopping, cooking, doing the laundry, and reparations. They keep the care recipient company, take him or her on excursions, walks, or visits to others, and generally see to it that all is well. Giving care is normal in the civil society. Its occurrence in the civil society should not be interpreted as a sign that the publicly operated social system in Sweden has failed or is lacking in resources. Nor should it be seen as a sign that the commercial market for care giving in Sweden is underdeveloped or has failed.

For those cases which the civil society cannot assist, care provided by public agencies or purchased on the commercial market are necessary options. As we see, the care giving aspect of the civil society exists even in the most developed welfare state. Its norms are basically particularistic, and it embraces mainly those near and dear, not one and all, as in the public welfare system, whose norms are universalistic in principle. Universalistic norms are general and neutral. In cases governed by particularistic norms the relationships between individuals are all-encompassing (Parsons says "diffuse"): people help one another irrespective of what the assistance entails. An interesting question for research is how responsibility between particularistic and universalistic institutions is distributed in modern welfare states. It is not certain that Sweden has arrived at the optimal distribution.

Cases

The civil society can in the main provide caretaking of the type described above, not professional nursing or medical cures. Of the cases considered, 82 percent involve chronic problems for which no cure is in sight; care will be required for the remainder of their lives. It is noteworthy against this background that, on the whole, the careers in the civil society consider themselves capable of coping with their tasks. The million careers in today's Sweden would get more recognition for their contribution. Their work is hidden, and it is often lonely and unappreciated. One suspects that many need relief in the form of replacements some time during the week in order to see to their own daily needs. Many no doubt need a vacation. They also need understanding from their employers when they sometimes need to take time off from work or go home to handle a crisis situation that has arisen.

REFERENCES

Currie, Eliott, and Jerome H. Skolnick, 1984, *America's Problem* Boston: Little Brown and Company.

Dunn, William, 1986, *Policy Analysis: Perspectives, Concepts and Methods,* Greenwich, Ct: J.A.I Press.

Durkneim, Emile, 1958, *Socialism and Saint-Simon* (Le Socialisme) ed. by Alvin W. Gouldner, Ohio: Yellow Springs.

Erikson, Kai T 1962, "Notes on the Sociology of Deviance", *Social Problems, 9,*311 (Spring), reprinted in Howard S. Becker. ed., *The Other Side,* Glencoe: The Free Press, 1964, pp. 9-15.

CHAPTER 4

Towards Understanding NGOs

> NGOs have a significant role to play, alongside governments, in improving the status of women.
>
> —*Jenny Shipley*

Characterising NGDOs

Writers on organisations define what they are dealing with in different ways. In this book, the simplest method would be to declare that the organisations of concern are the non-governmental, non-profits involved in the aid system. Unfortunately, two negative (non this and that) and one positive criteria (part of the aid system) tell us nothing useful about NGDO characteristics. An alternative approach is to look widely at a variety of relevant organisations and search for common features. A drawback is that subsequent results can be strongly biased by the initial selection.' A further option is to begin with more general, abstract understandings of organisations and then narrow down the selection by progressively identifying features which correspond most closely to those being analysed.

This last method has been chosen for four main reasons. First, characteristics of NGDOs must include their function in society compared to other organisations. Second, the nature and roles of non-profits are so varied that without a preliminary framework for analysis, it is difficult to make sense of what is to be found across the world. Third, there is already a substantial amount of study on organisations in society, albeit biased towards business and public administration. It is therefore more sensible to take this work as a resource to build upon. Finally, managers will run their NGDOs more effectively if they have some basic principles to refer back to.

Working Definitions

Much of today's international development effort is directed at a variety of organisations and institutions - social change is seldom achieved by an individual acting alone. Understanding NGDOs therefore requires working definitions of these two terms.

Organisations and Institutions

Probably the most basic definition of organisations is that they are purposeful, role-bound social units. In other words, they are groups of individuals who allocate tasks between themselves to contribute to a common goal. This simple definition gets very muddled in practice because, for example, not everyone may share the goal to the same degree, or they may be in the organisation for personal reasons which have little or nothing to do with what the organisation wants to achieve. Despite these complications, the two items to bear in mind are: to exist an organisation needs a purpose; and an organisation is made up of people who know what their role is (what is expected of them in relation to each other, in order to reach the purpose). The significance of purpose, or mission, in organisational life makes this a common starting point for subdivision or classification. A more difficult classification is between organisation and institution, terms which are, incorrectly, used interchangeably in today's development jargon.

Where organisations themselves, or where principles or norms of people's behaviour, become a stable, accepted and collectively valued basis on which society works, we can talk of social institutions. However, not all organisations become institutions and not all institutions are made up of organisations, which can be confusing. For example, marriage is a valued social institution which is not made up of organisations. Similarly, money is a valued social institution, but it cannot be equated to the behaviour of all banks, insurance companies or the Treasury. Corruption can also become institutionalised in some societies as the only way of getting things done, but this pattern of behaviour is not typical of one place or one organisation.

Some organisations can become institutionalised in the sense that they are a recognised and valued part of society. In the context of Great Britain, Oxfam has become such a household name that it is itself institutionalised. The same can probably be said for the Fundacion Sociale in Colombia, United Way in the USA, the Bangladesh Rural Advancement Committee (BRAC) and the Red Cross. By and large. NGDOs seldom make an adequate distinction between development of organisations and social institutions, which means that their strategies and methods are often not optimal, While there is no water tight distinction, an NGDO needs to be clear about these two terms, because they are not interchangeable and affect the way things have to be done. Nevertheless, even if the intended impact is institutional, organisations are the most common operational focus of development work and therefore remain the primary subject of this book.

Formal and Informal Organising

Before identifying specific characteristics of NGDOs, it is necessary to highlight a common short-sightedness in much Western analysis of organisations and institutions; this is the tendency to overlook what is not formally organised and legally recognised by governments. While informal organisations are found across the world, a significant feature of organisational life in countries of the South and East is that they rely on interpersonal networks. These networks are familial and customary rather than enshrined in organisational constitutions, and can be very powerful in shaping how both organisations and institutions work in practice.

There is a rich array of non-legalised forms of organised co-operation that people create to achieve shared goals; these may be formal for those belonging inside them, even if outsiders see them as informal. Age sets are an example common throughout sub-Saharan Africa, as are the *pakikisama* affiliations in the Philippines. As governments retreat, opening space for civic initiatives, the number and density of both informal and legally formal ways of collaborating is growing rapidly. While the merits of non-formalised organising should not be over-idealised, it would be very wrong, especially in the work of people-centred development, to remain unaware of the resource significance and demands which this type of growth makes on the work of all development agencies.

Organisational Sectors and Their Principles

Purpose is a common way of differentiating between types of organisations. Past study indicates that the evolution of societies as modern nation-Mates gives rise to institutions and organisations established for three relatively distinct purposes;

- to protect, secure and regulate the lives and actions of citizens; for example, to manage how society is defended as well as how it functions and progresses:
- to make a livelihood and create and accumulate wealth, and accumulate wealth; and
- to purse individual interests or tackle personal or social concerns which are separate from gaining a livelihood.

The first set of purposes typically belongs to governments, the second to business and the market, and the third to the self-willed association of citizens. Organisational science uses a shorthand of first, second and third sectors as labels for these purposes.

The sectors themselves can be divided into whether the purpose they serve is private or public. The first sector is concerned with what is called the public realm, that is the common area allotting all citizens in which they have rights and obligations, both of which are enforced by government agencies. The second sector makes up the private realm of people's initiatives to survive and improve economically; the third makes up the private realm for the pursuit of recreational, spiritual, social, cultural, and other personal or collective interests.

In reality, the three -way spilt is confused by the fact that private organisations can play a similar role to governments when they are established for public purposes. For example, rais occurs when a voluntary organisation is set up to serve some common good - such as, helping the aged, or assisting people whose rights base been abided. In addition, establishing a business or a non-profit is an act of free will: society does not expect or require any one private organisation to exist or be around for ever: this is not the case with government. Choosing to gam social recognition by formal registration means accepting society's right to oversee that you do what you say you will. In other words, registration is accepting obligations of public accountability which society determines and regulates.

An important division within third sector purposes, therefore, is whether the organisation is established to serve others or to benefit those within it. This distinguishes between third-party public service providers and self-help or mutual-benefit organisations. The former delivers something to others, the latter is there for the benefit of its own members. A charity can be created to provide clean water to poor household (third parties) while an antateur football team or choir provides mutual benefits for the players or singers. Being either a service or mutual benefit organisation affects how they work.

Comparing Operating Principles

To understanding the organisational dimensions of NGDOs, it is helpful to compare the basic operating principles of these three sectors. This will enable us to identify features which are supposed to make voluntary organisations particularly suited to people-centred development work.

People in Organisations

How do you get people to behave well in their organisational roles? Studies suggest that people behave the way they need to in organisations either: because they have to, that is. they are coerced; because they have incentives to do so, they are induced: or they are driven to do so by their own internal beliefs and values. At the risk of gross generalisation, each of the three sectors is found to adopt a different way of ensuring that people behave effectively in their roles: governments tend to rely on hierarchy, command and enforcement; businesses provide (or deny) monetary and other rewards as incentives; voluntary organisations rely on personal values, commitment and self-motivation.

While elements of each type of motivation can surely be found in all organisations, an important consequence of self-motivation in third-sector organisations is that individuals feel empowered to behave like co-owners, with a corresponding expectation to be treated in such a way by management; this impacts on organisational culture and decision-making processes. Of course, a person's technical competence, experience, aptitudes, personal situation, and aspirations are also important for fulfilling a role effectively. But the basic way an organisation goes about motivating all these elements within an individual is distinct for each sector.

Relating to the Outside World

Organisations in each sector tend to differ in how they relate to the outside world, particularly towards those they are supposed to serve. Governments, because of their public role and unique position of power, are inclined to be authoritative in their dealings with citizens; this may be tempered by setting standards for and soliciting feedback on the performance of public services. Further, the state-citizen relationship is effectively tied within a permanent set of mutual obligations which are, or should be, negotiated through the political process. Governments are also empowered to legislate and enforce; in this way they create much of the environment in which they operate.

Private businesses seldom have permanent relationships with their owners or customers from birth to death, although banks and insurance companies may get close to it. The relationship between business and their customers is overwhelmingly based on momentary transactions called purchases - the universal process of buying, selling, or bartering. Lacking formal coercive power, businesses try to condition the external world through advertising, by building monopolies and by, occasionally, employing corrupt practices or attempting to coerce customers into buying from them. Without legislative power to contract the environment in which they operate, enterprises try to protect their internal functioning from external disruption - such insulation is particularly necessary for mass production lines and processes which transform physical resources into products.

In addition, businesses are concerned to maintain their image of reliability, quality and corporate social responsibility, where advertising and media events play an important role. However, left to their own devices without public controls or incentives, competition naturally inclines businesses to minimise the internal costs and externalise the public costs of their activity -such as environmental degradation or pollution to tax payers.

Voluntary sector organisations do not have the legislative capability and coercive force of the state nor the economic clout of commercial capital and enterprise. What they have, instead is the dynamism and power of self-willed human action, which can encompass very large numbers of people and exert significant influence in society, is seen in civic protests or consumer boycotts. In as far as voluntary organisations are set up by value-driven, self-motivated people to serve a segment of the population unreached by the state or market, there is a strong identification between the organisation and those it is set up for. In NGDO jargon, this is termed solidarity. Groups or classes with particular interests can go so far as to set up non-profit organisations to gain political power - for example, establishing themselves as political parties.

The duration of relationships between voluntary

organisations and the individuals they serve differs widely. For member-based institutions, such is organised religion, the relationship is usually permanent. For others, such as social and recreational organisations, membership is unlikely to be permanent but may span a number of years. For historical and legal reasons, non-membership voluntary organisations are usually most active in providing public goods with a social benefit, such as education, health and welfare. Interactions with clients, therefore, tend, on balance, to be more than momentary but seldom permanent, which orients third-sector organisations towards transactions which could last from days to years, but where the idea of eventual separation is understood from the start.

Looking back to the goals and tasks of development, it is clear that NGDOs can hardly be in the business of selling services to those in poverty. If the poor could pay the full cost, the market, in theory, would respond to satisfy their demand. Moreover, the actual process of 'producing' development is rooted within communities themselves, which means that NGDOs must negotiate in order to integrate their work with ongoing external processes. How they can do this well is the subject of other chapters, where we will see that an NGDO's ability to negotiate is related to its attitude or stance, as expressed through the staff who do the negotiating. In its turn, organisational stance depends on the degree to which the voluntary sector has a vibrant presence. It also depends on the ability to mobilise appropriate financial resources, and here again there are sectoral differences.

Resource Mobilisation

Each organisational sector mobilises resources in different ways. While shareholders and banks provide capital, a business stands or falls on its ability to sell goods and services to customers for an amount sufficiently greatger than their cost; if not, bankruptcy results. By and large, non-membership voluntary organisations do not recover the full cost of what they provide to their clients or beneficiaries; and this is certainly the case for NGDOs who, on an ongoing basis, have to raise finances from other sources, loosely termed donors. In the case of international development, most NGDOs fulfil an intermediary role in a chain which generates and transfers resources: knowledge, technology, money, information. The NGDO task is to add value to the transfer process. For the present, it is sufficient to point out that being located between donors in one continent and stakeholders in another, or between affluent urban-based financiers and geographically remote, impoverished and socially marginalised beneficiaries, presents particular difficulties for management; these difficulties are further aggravated by the fact that performance is not easy to measure.

Feedback and Performance

What constitutes a 'bottom line for each sector? How can an organisation find out how well it is doing.' What feedback provides such information? For governments, or better said the regime in power, the bottom line is political the level of citizen satisfaction expressed through the ballot box or through civil disobedience, unrest and riots. For example, refusal to pay local government service charges in South Africa was one way that disenfranchised citizens could express dissatisfaction with services to their townships. Imperfect as they may be, existing democratic systems and public feedback - expressed through civic action, constituents' letters, petitions and percentages of the vote - do periodically focus politicians' minds and call them to account.

While arguments are raised to include corporate social responsibility as an element of performance, the bottom line for businesses remains that of profitability. Market indicators, such as share value, price/earnings ratios and market share, while obviously open to differences in interpretation, provide effective and immediate feedback to managers.

In the voluntary sector, when it comes to performance measures and feedback, there is a significant difference between the two kinds of organisation - mutual benefit and service - we identified earlier. In the former, performance measures and feedback can be readily gained from those who should be reaping the benefits. In formal set-ups, this process is usually built into the governance system of annual meetings and members' voting rights, while informal organisations select their own ways to provide information on whether or not members are getting what they want.

For most third-sector service-providing organisations, on the other hand, no straightforward, uncontented performance measures present themselves. The nearest we can come to a bottom line is credibility and legitimacy, measures which must to be 'constructed' from the combined social judgement of the organisation's many "users', including intended beneficiaries, governors, volunteers and staff. This is a complicated way of going about things, lacks the immediacy of the market, is open to dispute because users are seldom of equal weight, and makes comparisons or 'benchmarking' very difficult. The lack of clear performance indicators makes the management of non-profits more complex and difficult than other sectors.

For third-sector service providers in general, and for NGDOs specifically, the most critical line of feedback and measure must come from the primary stakeholder (this term is increasingly used instead of clients, beneficiary or target group), because it is their poverty or deprivation which is used to justify the organisation's existence. Changes in the well being of the primary stakeholders must be reported back to donors. Unfortunately, this line of feedback is usually very weak and is seldom able to influence an NGDO's overall performance; all too often. NGOs prefer to fulfill pre-defined project activities which qualify for further financing. Relative inattention to long-term impact means that feedback on working with communities does not gain equal weight with pressures coming down the aid chain from constituents and donors.

Comparative Advantages of the Third Sector in People-Centred Development

It is commonly assumed, and argued strongly by NGDOs, that their place within the voluntary (third) sector, and the principles which go with it, give them comparative advantages.

What are the arguments supporting this view? First, value-driven, committed and self-motivated staff should mure readily identify with and be able to adopt an appropriate stance towards their clients, engendering trust and enhancing authentic participation. In comparison, and irrespective of the individual or their technical function, government staff always carry with them the status of power, limiting their ability to identify with the poor or to be accepted by them. It certainly confines their ability to support empowerment processes when such processes are directed against government itself.

Second, NGDOs do not need the uniformity or standardisation of practices which state bureaucracies apply; as a result, they can adapt more, readily to local contexts and meet the demands of people centred development. They can organise themselves to provide tailored support to a particular disadvantaged group -unmarried mothers, the landless, people with AIDS, the non-credit worthy, or the disabled. In other words, they are better able to target their assistance, which should improve efficiency and effectiveness. Third, while commercial organisations can adapt themselves to their clients' needs, they are not particularly interested in and cannot reach, the really poor in the way NGDOs can because of donor support (which could be called a form of subsidy): such support is only forthcoming because of die trust in their non-profit principles. Fourth. NGDOs are not a public body, giving them the flexibility to stay long enough to help make a difference, but not so long that dependency results Governments, on the other hand, are there for ever. Fifth, in not seeking profits, NGDOs can be less costly than business, while staff self-motivation enables them to function at less than market rates because part of the employee's reward comes from self-fulfilment. Finally, NGDOs can undertake necessary development functions and supporting processes which are not 'services' as such.

These functions can entail, for example, providing a channel for information and other types of 'bridges' between different types of organisation, facilitating links, acting as a catalyst and temporarily filling gaps: such activities are effectively impossible to measure and difficult to classify as a service, but important none the less. Because of their principles. NGDOs are less likely to face the accusation of creating work simply to profit owners, a common complaint made against service-contracting companies, such as consultancy firms, which are driven to sell staff time.

While the validity of these arguments may be questioned, in theory at least, applying voluntary sector principles should be positive in terms of development effectiveness. The next step is to trace what happens when organisational theory moves into today's development practice.

Understanding NGDO's

The three sectors described above are imaginary, they are unlikely to be found exactly like this in the real world. But this framework helps to describe NGDOs and why they behave as they do. identifying underlying forces which must he dealt with in practical organisation and management. When the different principles of each sector overlap within an organisation, however, problems can result.

The overall purpose of NGDOs and the typical tasks and critical balances involved in being effective. Attention should now be focused on what happens to people-centred development in an increasingly contract-oriented aid system. In other words, what challenges arise to NGDO management and organisation when they have to operate in the more complicated areas of overlapping principles?

Rather than dealing with mutual benefits and other types of organisations within the voluntary sector, this discussion concentrates on service-providing NGDOs. One observation is that organisations located firmly within the third sector, and consistently applying its principles, are most likely to be supplying welfare-type services. Like the Lions and Rotary clubs, they may be composed of unpaid volunteers, occasionally raising donations from well-wishers, or they may have evolved into more stable charitable institutions, providing homes for destitute children or people with disabilities. While beneficial, this type of activity is not what today's empowering people-centred development is thought to be about and, consequently, such voluntary organisations, although sometimes recipients of aid, are not the focus of this book.

Instead, the third-sector organisations of primary interest are those operating within the framework of objectives and tasks set out. Today, evidence suggests that these voluntary organisations are more likely to be found in areas of overlap *2,* 3 and 4 than in V. Why?' The answer is as follows: over a period of 30 years the aid system has become an aid business demanding a high degree of professionalism from NGDOs, displacing moral motivations with more functional concerns of effective delivery. International assistance, furthermore, is increasingly assigned on the basis of project-based competitive contracts. Aid priorities are shifting away from governments, reallocating what were once state responsibilities for public services into the other two sectors; this has lead to more NGDO tax-based funding. Structural adjustment policies have decreased spending on public services, creating a 'moral' pressure on NGDOs to fill the gup and a dilemma on whether or not they should do so. There is a stagnation in the growth of private donations to development work, and the proportion of NGDO funds derived From official aid donors is rapidly increasing. To appreciate what all this means in terms of effects and challenges, we must look at what is likely to happen to the comparative advantages of voluntary development as the different sectoral principles overlap.

Overlaps between sectors can work in tuo directions. For example, business can combine its principles with those of the voluntary sector by, for example, creating non-monetary incentives as a motivation for staff. Conversely, in the voluntary sector values of participation and empowerment can be combined with the material rewards common to business in how staff want to be rewarded. Current trends are towards the latter rather than the former, so our concentration is on how government and business principles overlap and affect the management and organisation of NGDOs.

What might occur within NGDOs when they provide

public services similar to the state (area 2), which many do? For a start, staff may be inclined to behave in directive ways, treating those they serve simply as recipients who should be happy with whatever level of service they get. Put another say, solidarity is an unlikely attitude. The NGDO may start to believe that it has a right to an everlasting place in society, putting its own interests above the continual need to demonstrate its credibility, with staff expecting permanent employment. Arguing that it is doing the government's job, NGDOs will make claims on public funds which - without sufficient care - bring with them conditions and expectations that the organisation will operate in accordance with government standards, practices and political needs. In short, the NGDO functions as a parastatal agency in all but name. This behaviour is observed in India, where the government has allocated large sums of money for NGDOs to assist an implementing the National Development Plan.

Where NGDO functions are overlapped by businesses principles, NGDOs may adopt the ethos of entrepreneurs and contractors. Poverty alleviation and humanitarian relief may change from being a moral response to a social problem, turning poor people into a 'product' to be marketed and sold. Market position, in terms of the organisation's share in private and public aid donations, becomes a dominant concern, leading to fund-raising practices which overstate achievements or which, in pursuit of a sympathetic response from donors, distort information or present images which may do an injustice to those for whom the NGDO operates.

Growth and the ability to spend, rather than the profitability of the company, become criteria for measuring success; the legitimate difficulties of performance measurement may be used to hide shortcomings in development impact. Transparency in operations also suffers because failures or set-backs are treated as potentially bad publicity and therefore unwelcome news, instead of a source of learning. As a consequence, internal systems which seek to monitor or evaluate performance are viewed as a contract imposition and their outputs are not made available to the public, which undermines accountability.

Increasing market profile and income share is a now a common concern of Northern NGDOs' fund-raising; overstating impact is wide-spread; distortions in fund-raising images are a frequent complaint of NGDOs from the South and East; and the lack of transparency is a source of growing disquiet in development circles and the media.

Commercial companies continually search for ways to reduce costs, especially by applying economics of scale. NGDOs may do the same in order to save donor funds, but at the cost of diseconomies of development processes and wilful ignoring of indirect effects. For example, an NGDO involved in supporting school construction throughout a country in East Africa negotiated with communities that when they had built the walls, the NGDO would provide the roofing materials. To save money, materials were bought in bulk from one supplier. But the centralised purchasing arrangements bore no relationship to the varied stages of interaction with communities. The rains came before materials arrived, and in some cases substantial damage occurred to the new classrooms. Result? Community demotivation and economic waste. Simply put, economies of scale come at the cost of choice and flexibility. NGDOs must therefore be able to make difficult trade-offs setting desirable economic optimisation against effectiveness in complex development processes.

What the business overlap also brings is a greater concern to control costs and ensure sound financial management. As long as these aspects are applied in ways which do not undermine or limit the application of best development practice, they constitute a significant benefit to NGDOs who are often lax in these areas, partly because business approaches have not been seen as consistent with a culture of solidarity. Part of appropriate NGDO professionalism must include attention to costs and benefits and ensuring proper use of financial resources; business can offer useful experience and guidance, but is not necessarily as pre-packaged methods.

Financial incentives are needed to gain professional staff; however, this runs counter to the spirit of voluntarism and self-motivation and the organisational culture which goes with it. The introduction of a competitive culture creates organisational tensions, conflicts of conscience and personal stress, especially for middle managers. For example, it is argued that hierarchy, which is accepted as normal in government and business, increases effective decision-making, while committed staff, who are prepared to forego a market rate for their labour in NGDOs expect democratic decision processes as well as the right to influence policy and practice; this expectation leads to -'paralysis of participation'. How are the two to be balanced? Finally, pressure to compete can sway NGDOs' attentions towards donors as primary stakeholders, rather than towards those who provide their legitimacy. Put another way, the service given to the donor becomes more important than the benefit to those who justify the NGDO's existence.

It is easy to sec that area 4 is a position of great complexity, calling for NGDOs to juggle with and balance three different sets of principles at once. They must contribute to sustained poverty alleviation and social justice using their voluntary attributes, while functioning as businesses to provide public services. This is obviously not a desirable position, but sometimes it cannot be avoided, particularly in conditions of severe economic decline, ineffectual governments and high levels of national dependency on aid as, for example, in Burundi, Malawi, Mozambique, Mauritania, Nepal and Sierra Leone. In these settings, NGDOs must operate as very complicated hybrids, with the potential to suffer from all the tensions and unwelcome effects described above. NGDO organisation and management must actively counter the problems arising from multiple operating principles at the risk of otherwise becoming completely ineffective. Governments and businesses are seldom confronted with such situations and therefore have little to offer in terms of proven solutions.

Overall, while varying in degree between and within continents, opportunistic business and government behaviour continues to confuse the voluntary sector. An entrepreneurial shift in the aid market place leads to the NGDO label being appropriated by a variety of participants. Lip service is paid to voluntarism and solidarity. The overriding concern becomes survival at all costs.

The often less than Haltering - acronyms used across the world for organisations which claim to be NGDOs but are not inspired by the principles and values of voluntarism. One long-term observer asserts that NGDOs are, in fact, no longer part of the third sector, but belong in the second because their practices show that market, rather than voluntary, values dominate. The question this poses, and a concern of this book, is how can NGDOs reposition themselves to regain and apply the principles of development voluntarism in a commercial world?

Re-establishing NGDOs Within the Voluntary Sector

The past five years have seen significant tensions and upheavals occurring within NGDOs as the tectonic plates of voluntary, government and business principles collide with each other. In geology, such collisions result in a new landscape or, in some cases, ongoing instability with occasional earthquakes and eruptions. The NGDO landscape is still tar from suible, but there are signs that without conscious counter measures it will settle, Uphoft has argued, outside the third sector. This would be a misfortune. Northern NGDOs have tended to adopt two distinct strategies in the struggle to introduce and somehow reconcile different sets of organisational principles. Some have embarked on massive and painful organisation-wide processes of reorientation, commonly labelled restructuring.

Others have tried to change organisational culture and practices from above by importing chief executives and senior managers from the business world. Some have done both. There has been a common trend to redirect, streamline and increase the impact of operations by embarking on strategic planning, a still ongoing process for many NGDOs which has seldom been part of their management repertoire. What this activity entails in practice is an important topic of the next chapter. In the South, NGDOs have also been facing the dual challenge of repositioning themselves in a new aid context, as well as adjusting to the installation of democracy, especially in Latin America, sub-Saharan Africa and the old Communist block. The responses have been steered by ideology, donor pressure and local opportunities. Soul-searching internal reviews, accompanied by difficult dialogues with Northern counterparts, have been undertaken by many of the larger organisations, such as IBASE in Brazil, DESCO in Peru and by the sound of it, almost all within the NGDO community in Chile. Repositioning through strategic planning is becoming a preoccupation with Southern NGOs, partly as a consequence of the strategic choices made by Northern supporters; these will be examined later. In the East, local NGDOs are a recent organisational arrival; there is often confusion about their legal standing, especially if the regimes in power are unsure of what autonomy they can or want to tolerate. An example is Kazakstan, where recent constitutional amendments have curtailed possible areas of NGDO activity.

The major challenge to NGDOs in finding a social position in Eastern countries is not the pressure that arises from overlapping sectors. Rather, difficulties arise in forming a socially recognised, stable third sector in post-authoritarian states - in a context where long-term support from the North is uncertain and inadequate. However, despite differences within and between continents, one agenda that is emerging for some NGDOs of the South and East which rely on aid looks for long-term strategies which tie NGDOs more firmly to their own economies.

All in all, NGDOs are in the midst of a severe identity crisis. The issue is to determine how NGDOs can emerge from this period so that voluntary values, principles and development advantages co-exist with, but are not made subordinate to, those of business and the market. Some would argue that it is too late; NGDOs as we knew them have already lost their soul. The immediate task is to examine what, in organisational and management terms, can be done to re-establish a position which embodies voluntarism in practice as well as in name.

Regaining Identity Within Voluntarism

Retaining a position somewhere within the voluntary sector means ensuring that voluntary values and principles remain dominant in the context of a non-profit market place. Making this happen will depend on the nature and strength of an NGDO's identity, which in its rum is determined by consistency in the beliefs of those who govern its organisational values. Simply put, identity is determined by power over organisational philosophy and its translation into action.

Examining values and power in NGDOs is not straightforward because the first is highly abstract and the second seldom transparent. We will start with the most fundamental element of NGDO identity, its beliefs. Beliefs are the foundation for organisational values and philosophy of action. Together, beliefs, values and development philosophy form the reference point for what an NGDO is and stands for. They are the measure against which the organisation must judge itself and be judged by others.

Here, the lowest common denominator is that some individuals cared enough about some aspect of society to form an organisation to change things. For NGDOs which think no further than what they do, identity is equal to activity. In the aid system, this means that an organisation is no more than the project it runs. In other words, what the NGDO does equals what it is. In organisational and management terms, clear values and a philosophy are essential for effectiveness because they link an NGDO's purpose, policies, strategic aims and operational choices (discussed in the next chapter). Beliefs, vision and values are at the top of a hierarchy of organisational features which need to be in place if lower levels of organisational activity are to be done well. Without these 'foundations', serious inconsistencies between policies and real-life practices can and do arise. For example, while an NGDO believes that war veterans have a right to national respect and adequate economic support, their actual activities amount to little more than distributing hand outs, such as food and blankets. The inconsistency between the is not seen or is simply accepted for reasons organisational survival.

Is it chance that so few NGDOs have clear statements of the beliefs which inform their values and purpose? Not really. Most NGDOs are adverse to reaching this level of agreement; if such a statement is made, it appears that a creed must be followed. Better to leave things implicit than face contention and futile debate. This pragmatic view has, however, the drawback of avoiding issues which are critical to interpreting events and making consistent choices in unpredicted circumstances. One of the most important negative consequences is that a lack of shared beliefs and values reduces internal trust, leading to top-down, control-orientation which lessens an NGDOs ability to respond rapidly, to adapt to diversity or to adopt the truly participatory practices needed in interaction with primary stakeholders.

In addition to beliefs, the origins of NGDOs are important to their identity and with similarities and difference; between North, South and East. Northern NGDOs have arisen:

- from political affiliations;
- from the motivations of social groupings;
- for the promotion;
- to tackle specific issues, such as the environment;
- to advance technological solutions to problems;
- to promote particular ideologies;
- to support similar organisations;
- from personal inspiration.

In their many combinations, these different origins lead to a wide diversity in organisations giving each a unique identity as well as a tendenry to ensure that their individuality is maintained.

A similar list of origins applies to Southern NGDOs, but

with added historical and social dimensions. For Southern NGDOs, an important additional feature contributing to thyeir identity is past domination by foreign powers, which is still to be found in new guises. Hussein Adam has identified three common identity-shaping responses, of Southern NGDOs to their colonial histories which he terms, 'return to the past', 'seize the future' and "transmission belt'. The first, exemplified by the Six-S movement in West Africa and the Savadoya movement in Sri Lanka, seeks to rehabilitate and build upon the cultural or religious norms which were negated by colonisers and to use them as the well-spring of people-centred development action. Identity is closely associated with indigenous values. 'Seize the future' NGDOs react against past and present exploitation within and between countries. NGDOs within the anti-*dependencia* movement of Latin America, such as IBASE in Brazil, and others associated with communist movements in Asia, such as the People's Organisation for Participation (POP) in Thailand, find identity, amongst others, from their structural analysis of continuing domination, exploitation and denial of fundamental rights within their society and beyond. Identity is essentially defined in terms of an ideological position. As the name implies, 'transmission belts" provide that function through the transfer of aid resources. Identity derives from their role somewhere in the aid chain and the services they deliver. In other words, who they are is what they do.

In addition to colonial exploitation and injustice; NGDOs in the South and East can arise from struggles against internal oppression such as military or civilian dictators. Often informed by ideologies from the left (including theological interpretations of the Catholic church) and allied to revolt by peasants and farmers, NGDOs have been established by individuals and groups who may have been driven underground, or adopted other forms of resistance. Examples may be readily found in South East Asia and Latin America. But in response to such threats, in order to show that they are concerned about the plight of the poor, dictatorial regimes have been known to form, allow or promote certain NGDOs too. In either case, NGDO origins arise from, and mirror, a context of indigenous oppression. All in all it is not safe to look at the identity of NGDOs devoid of context or history.

The mix of values, philosophy and origins described above all contribute to the content of NGDO identity, but not necessarily to its strength or stability under pressure. Resilience in identity depends on how widely and consistently beliefs, values, development philosophy and organisational principles are shared between key groups.

A crude division governing identity can be made between an NGDO's formal 'owners': those recognised as accountable in law; its constituency: the organisation's social base; the leadership: the chief executive and senior management; and the staff at different levels. All groups exert power in their own way and to a different degree. Where significantly different perceptions about beliefs, purpose or principles arise, identity can become fragmented. For example, splits within the NGDO community and within an NGDO like the Philippines Peasant Institute can partly be attributed to widening differences in the political interpretation of the function and identity of NGDOs in the post-Marcos, post-Cold War era. Whether or not splits occur depends on the balance of power between the groups, the type of governing structure, and personalities and communication - where the chief executive's role is often pivotal.

There are three common governing structures: self-regulated, with or without membership: self-selected oligarchy; and constituent based. Much of Latin America conforms to the first type. The civic code under which NGDOs register creates a governing body composed of staff representatives, which can be expanded to include outsiders but this does not have to occur. In this sense, the staff who make up the organisation also own it; in effect, they own themselves and lack a social constituency with formal power. While differences in opinion can exist, in this set-up communication between owners and staff should not pose a problem. Organisational identity is likely to be strong and coherent, unless confidence is lost in the leadership. The drawbacks of this circular or incestuous set-up for public accountability and for dealing with contentious organisational change, such as reducing staff, are examined later.

In the rest of the world a more common structure is a governing board which is self-selected in perpetuity - an oligarchy. Staff and volunteers can be allocated places, but the majority of power rests with outsiders chosen by each other for their social position, political links, expertise, representative status or other beneficial attributes. In these circumstances, significant differences arising between board, leadership and staff on how to respond to pressures on voluntary principles can lead to public wrangling, long-term instability, demotivation and seriously reduced effectiveness. Less frequent, but not uncommon, are constituency-governed NGDOs. Constituency is an umbrella term for identifiable political and economic group(s) in society which the organisation stems from and relates to strongly. In the North, secular NGDOs with constituent assemblies are MS in Denmark and NOVIB in the Netherlands, the overseas development arms of trade unions to be found in Canada, and Amnesty International. NGDOs funded through child sponsorship, such as Plan International, ACTIONAID, World Vision, Christian Children's Funds and the Save the Children Funds, can readily point to a constituency or social base, but are not governed by them. With slight variations, these NGDOs have self-selected boards and only one includes representatives from countries of operation. which means the South and East are not formally represented; this can give an imbalance in interests served towards funders.

If the system of governance allows them to do so, NGDOs with a broadly-based, clearly definable constituency are more likely to be held to their founding principles and voluntary values than those which do not; members will have to be persuaded that the convictions they adhere to no longer hold. However, constituents' ability to exercise control in practice is largely determined by the information made available to inform their position. And here, leadership and staff usually have the upper hand, which can, and often docs, reduce any governing body to a rubber stamp. What one commonly observes is NGDO leaders and staff shaping and shifting identity.Too frequently boards end up taking remedial rather than preventive action.

How NGDOs go about re-establishing organisational identity when it becomes confused, contested or lost is dealt with in the next chapter. The point to conclude with here is that irrespective of the formal systems of governance, identity boris down to the integrity and honesty with which leaders and staff adhere to voluntary values and founding principles.

What Characterises NGDOs on Today's Development Scene?

The previous pages have been a long route to characterising the sort of organisations which are the subject of this book. What the approach illustrates is that it is possible to describe these organisations in positive ways without having to resort to the double negatives of non-profit and non-governmental. But what does this tell us about the essential characteristics of third-sector organisations and of the organisational and management features of development-oriented agencies?

Non-Governmental Organisations

The formal organisations making up the third sector differ from governments and businesses in that:

- They are not established for and cannot distribute any surplus they generate as a profit to owners or staff.
- They are not required nor prevented from existing by law, but result from people's self-chosen voluntary initiative to pursue a shared interest or concern.
- Formed by private initiative, they are independent, in that they are not part of government nor controlled by a public body.
- Within the terms of whatever legislation they choose to register themselves, they also govern themselves.
- Registration means that the founders wish to have

social recognition; this calls for some degree of formalisation and acceptance of the principle of social accountability.

Obviously, these basic criteria cover a vast array of organisations in any society, ranging from the Ku Klux Klan, through churches, amateur football teams, societies for the blind and physically handicapped, foundations for cancer research, ethnic welfare associations, the Ramblers Association, and the Salvation Army. In addition, there is a socially significant set of third-sector organisations which do not seek recognition in a formal sense, but may nevertheless be developmentally important.

Within this definition, how do NGOs dedicated to international development, distinguish themselves?

Non-Governmental Development Organisations

NGDOs are a subset of organisations within the five voluntary sector criteria listed above, but do not necessarily operate solely on the basis of voluntary sector principles. In terms of their particular characteristics:

- Within the framework of international cooperation. NGDOs are legitimised by the existence of the world's poor and powerless and by the circumstances and injustices they experience.
- By and large, NGDOs act as intermediaries, providing support to those who legitimise them; they are not mutual benefit organisations or associations.
- NGDOs are predominantly hybrid in nature, operating on the basis of multiple, partially conflicting, partially re-enforcing organisational principles.
- Realising effective sustainable development is critically dependent on NGDOs retainingvoluntary values and principles as the primary force in their way of working.

NGDOs face a particular set of challenges which require

appropriate organisation and skilled management if they are to be competent agents of development. What are they?

Organisational and Management Balances Faced by NGDOs

The organisational trade-offs and balances which NGDOs must achieve to be effective can be grouped under three main headings: the nature of voluntarism; the dynamics of the development scene, and the nature of social change in a world becoming dominated by market-driven economics and liberal political systems. As with development work, balancing does not mean equalising, but continually adjusting and managing the mix of internal and external forces to ensure that, overall, voluntarism overlaps government and business principles (rather than the other way round).

The Nature of Voluntarism

When maintaining voluntary principles, NGDOs will have to:

- Balance and ensure consistency between potentially conflicting claims on organisational ownership and values.
- Balance a third-sector governance style with market-oriented standards.
- Balance an organisational culture of voluntarism with that of competitive contracting and public service.
- Balance volunteer and staff self-motivation and commitment with market-related incentives and expectations.
- Balance staff participation and empowerment with directive decision-making.
- Balance between trust versus control in the allocation and application of authority.

The Development Scene

When operating in the system of international development co-operation, NGDO's will need to:

- Balance individual identity with NGDO collective interests and collaboration with other sectors.
- Balance accountability to primary stakeholders with credibility towards constituency and contributors.
- Balance the resource mix to ensure retention of autonomy in decision-making.
- Balance market-related and development-related performance criteria and demands.
- Balance the needs and standards of participatory development processes with tor-profit approaches to cost effectiveness and accounting.

Social Change

When pursuing processes of social change, NGDOs will have to:

- Balance competencies in service provision with competencies which cause structural change in society.
- Balance operating within market forces with changing how the market operates.

REFERENCES

Benveniste, Guy, 1984, "On a code of Ethics for Policy *Experts", Journal of Policy Analysis and Management,* 3:561-572.

Erikson, Kai T 1962, "Notes on the Sociology of Deviance", *Social Problems, 9,*311 (Spring), reprinted in Howard S. Becker. ed., *The Other Side,* Glencoe: The Free Press, 1964, pp. 9-15.

MacRae, Duncan, and James Wilde, *1979, Policy Analysis for Public* Decisions, N. Scituate, Ma.: Duxbury.

CHAPTER 5

Major Characteristics of NGOs

When you have an accident, they will save their own people, and those who have worked with you or with the NGOs are left. Unfortunately, this happens always. It is not an excuse at all.

—*Boutros Boutros-Ghali*

Introduction

Non-governmental organisations (NGOs) embrace a wide array of agencies within and across different countries of the world. At their broadest, NGOs are simply agencies or groups which are different from government bodies. However, NGOs are distinctive in containing a voluntary component and because they do not operate for profit. Development NGOs are thus a category of NGOs defined by their purpose of providing development assistance. But even in development parlance, the term NGO is used to encompass a whole range of organisations which differ in size, function, and geographical location.

Thus, the term can be used to describe small, locally based, and loosely established voluntary and largely grass-roots types of associations, as well as large, national, and even transnational voluntary associations with formal constitutions, employing hundreds of staff. They may be engaged in relief, emergency, or longer-term development work or a mixture of all three. The term NGDO—non-governmental development organisation—is frequently used to describe the growing numbers of associations whose work is exclusively concerned with broader development concerns. A distinction is also commonly made between NGOs which originated in and have their home-base in the industrial countries, which are referred to as 'northern' or 'international' NGOs, and those which originate in and operate within developing countries, which are termed 'southern' NGOs.

Over the past quarter-century, and especially during the past two decades, there has been a rapid growth in the numbers of NGOs involved in development, in the numbers of people working for NGOs, and in the amount of money which flows into voluntary agencies working in relief and development. Perhaps the greatest growth has been in the thousands of new grass-roots organisations (sometimes referred to simply as 'groups', sometimes as 'people's organisations', as in the *Human Development Report 1993)* which have grown up locally—some extending no further than one or two villages. However, there has also been a rapid growth in larger indigenous NGOs in the south, as well as in the numbers of northern NGOs. During this period, a number of the older NGOs have changed their role, the most common change being a shift from an exclusive concern with relief and emergency work to a focus which embraces, or sometimes is exclusively concerned with, broader development issues (Korten, 1990b).

These trends, and closer examination of the characteristics of different groups, have led to a distinction that is now commonly made between intermediary, or secondary, and primary organisations. Indeed Carroll (1992), whose work in this field has been particularly influential, distinguishes further between grass-roots support organisations (GSOs) and membership support organisations (MSOs). On occasion this growth has led to a blurring of the differences between governmental and non-governmental, and even between non-profit and for-profit organisations.

Thus, in an increasing number of developing countries, it has now become common for government and state agencies or for politicians to set up their own 'non-governmental' organisations, while in industrial countries it is now common practice for governments to channel some of their aid funds to and through NGOs. Similarly, concern with longer-term survival has encouraged some NGOs to raise funds by establishing commercial-type ventures such as shops, stores, and mail-order facilities, while in Italy 'business NGOs' have been formed for the specific purpose of securing aid contracts from the Italian Government.

In some countries, NGOs have been established which are little more than advisory or consulting agencies to service the growing voluntary sector.

Northern NGOs

The number of northern development NGOs has increased rapidly in the 1980s. At the same time, there has been growing diversification and specialisation within the NGO community, reflecting the wide range of activities in which they are now engaged. As a result, it has become increasingly difficult to make generalisations about what northern NGOs do and about the particular role that they see for themselves in development. Within individual industrialised countries, NGOs operate within different legal systems and with different public expectation of their role.

However, in most countries there is a strong church-based link to at least one, and often more, of the major NGOs. Indeed, agencies affiliated to the Protestant and Catholic churches dominate the NGO sector in Denmark and Germany (where they account for two-thirds of private contributions), although most maintain a strict separation between and development work. In Germany, in addition to the large church-based NGOs, there are also the four political foundations which constitute an important element of the NGO community, promoting development within their explicit and different political objectives. Some important non-denominational NGOs whose interests include work on development were founded in the nineteenth and early twentieth centuries.

The British Anti-Slavery Society was established as far

back as 1823 and Save the Children Fund in 1919. Others were formed during and after World War II, initially with a focus on relief: Oxfam was founded in 1942 (Black, 1992), CARE (Co-operative Agency for Relief Everywhere) in 1945, War on Want in 1953, NOVIB in 1956, and Misereor in 1958. In the 1960s there was a major expansion in the number of development-focused NGOs, both secular and denominational. In the 1970s and on into the 1980s, new organisations were formed which had a more specific sectoral, technical, or geographical focus. One such in Britain, the Intermediate Technology Development Group, was founded as early as 1965.

Northern NGOs are principally engaged in funding development projects and providing food and other materials for disasters and emergencies. An important distinction is whether they are operational or not: operational agencies implement projects directly in developing countries using their own staff and resources, whereas non-operational agencies finance projects from their headquarters or regional office, often channelling funds through partner organisations with whom special relationships are frequently developed.

Large US-based NGOs like CARE, Plan International, and World Vision are all operational, as are ActionAid and Save the Children Fund in the UK. The trend, however, is away from hands-on involvement and towards working directly with indigenous NGOs. In Britain this is now common practice for agencies such as CAFOD (Catholic Fund for Overseas Development) and Christian Aid. Many NGOs tailor their approach to the situation in particular countries; thus, the non-operational approach is favoured more in South Asia and Latin America, whereas in many parts of Africa northern NGOs continue to be strongly interventionist.

Some northern NGOs, such as Oxfam, Save the Children Fund, Misereor, and NOVIB, have in-country offices which liaise with and offer support to indigenous NGOs in the form of training and exchange visits. Others, such as Christian Aid, have made a deliberate decision not to do so (Riddell, 1993), though recent changes have occurred in this policy.

In addition to providing financial support for development projects, many NGOs are involved in development education and advocacy work in their own countries. Indeed, distinct NGOs, like the Centre for World Development Education in England and Wales, have been set up in order to concentrate on such activities. However, emphasis on work in this area varies, and in a number of European countries, where a large share of funds come from the state, advocacy work receives a low priority.

While the statistics are known to be incomplete, OECD data suggest that there were 2,542 NGOs in the twenty-four OECD countries in 1990, compared with 1,603 in 1980 (OECD, 1990a). In addition, almost all NGOs grew in terms of funds and personnel during this period. Between 1980 and 1990, the total flow of private funds sent by northern NGOs to developing countries rose from S2.4bn. to $5.Ibn., rising eventually to $6.3bn. However, a relatively small group of large organisations predominate: some 200 NGOs (less than 10 per cent of the total) account for some three-quarters of the volume of grants to developing countries *(The Courier,* 1987). Absolute numbers and growth trends also conceal significant variation among countries: there are hundreds of NGOs in Canada, the USA, and northern European countries where NGOs have strong historical traditions and thrive on public philanthropy, and comparatively few in Mediterranean countries such as Greece and Portugal.

In Britain, the sector is dominated by a small group of large agencies: out of some 300 development NGOs, twelve account for over 80 per cent of total voluntary income, and seven of these had incomes in excess of £10m. in 1990. Oxfam is the largest in terms of turnover, followed by Save the Children Fund, Christian Aid, the World Wide Fund for Nature, ActionAid, Tear Fund, and CAFOD. Another fail recent development has been the creation of 2 number of specialist NGOs, which focus on specific constituencies, approaches to development, and sectors of activity. These include Water Aid, Health Unlimited, and the Intermediate Technology Development Group, while increased interest in the environment has raised the profile of the World Wide Fund for Nature.

Growth in the number and incomes of development NGOs in the industrialised countries has tended to raise their significance in relation to the total voluntary sector. Thus, in Britain, development NGOs account for approximately one-sixth of the total volume of funds raised by charities in the form of private contributions. There are two main reasons for this growth in size and numbers of northern NGOs. The first has been the increase in media exposure of famine and disasters, together with the more professional manner in which these issues have been presented. Not only has the role of NGOs been highlighted, the NGO BandAid owed its origins to public interest aroused by media coverage of the Ethiopian famine of the mid-1980s.

This provided a major stimulus for increased levels of private contributions, which appears to have been sustained into the early 1990s in spite of worries expressed within the NGO movement that a combination of 'aid fatigue' and the media dominance of problems in eastern Europe and the former Soviet Union would lead to a drop in public donations. More recently, however, contributions have begun to fall. A second set of factors contributing to NGO growth is related more to events outside the world of NGOs. One has been growing disillusion among official aid organisations about their own ability to alleviate poverty through their often large-scale rural development programmes. This has led, in part, to a switch in focus away from small and localised development projects to larger macro-political issues in official aid provision. Another factor has been the increasing prominence given to private initiatives in development.

These influences have not only combined to raise the profile and status of the voluntary-sector NGOs in development, but have also led to significant increases in the quantity of public money which government ministries and aid agencies have channelled to and through NGOs. Government funding grew at a faster rate than private contributions daring the 1980s. In the period 1980-8, official contributions increased in real terms by 55 per cent, as compared with 25 per cent for private contributions. By 1988 NGOs in the eighteen DAC member states raised $4.2bn. from private contributions but received $2.3bn. from official sources, giving a total of $6.3bn. By 1992 the total had risen to $8.8bn., though still equivalent to around 15 per cent of total official aid. In the period from 1970 to 1993, the total non-government funds of NGOs channelled to developing countries rose from $860m. to $6.3bn.

Yet as a share of total official aid there was a slight decline over this period—from 12.3 per cent in 1970 to 11 per cent in 1993. The most significant change over the past quarter of a century has been the growth of total NGO income coming from official aid sources. According to the World Bank (World Bank, 1995: 23), in 1970 official donors only provided about 1.5 per cent of total NGO income. But by 1992 the figure had risen to $2.5bn., and to account for some 30 per cent of total NGO income. The exact proportions vary markedly between individual countries.

Though, in some cases, the data are known (by the OECD) to be little more than crude estimates, and it has not been possible for some years to provide comprehensive data for eleven OECD donors, the best available country. For at least four donors, over 20 per cent of all official aid is now channelled to or through NGOs. Of importance, too, the data show that in the case of at least six countries, over 40 per cent of total NGO income comes from official aid sources. Besides these different forms of financial support to northern NGOs, some donors provide funds directly to southern NGOs, either bilaterally to individual organisations from aid headquarters or through diplomatic missions.

Canada has progressed furthest down this path. In 1987 it provided some S16m. to indigenous NGOs through aid missions in 115 countries. In a variant of this approach, USAID provides umbrella grants through its aid missions for use by US PVO's as well as indigenous NGOs (OECD, 1988: 91-3). The British Government has also started to fund local NGO activities, initially by supporting indigenous NGOs involved in family planning as part of a larger bilateral aid programme in Bangladesh. In 1994 a further new initiative began in east Africa, when ODA began a programme to fund the work of local NGOs directly with an initial budget of £l.'5m. (Riddell and Bebbington, 1995).

On the multilateral front, a significant channel for indigenous NGO funding is through the European Community's micro-project schemes, which in many Lome Convention countries are administered by an official paid for by the Community. Overall, however, this channel covers only a minor proportion of official aid allocated to NGOs. Both resistance on the part of some northern NGOs and the limited capacity of most aid missions to monitor small project grants have worked against any major shift in favour of direct funding.

Southern NGOs and Grass-Roots Organisations

While there has been a steady growth in the number and size of northern NGOs in the 1980s, there has been an explosion in the number of southern NGOs. For instance, there are now several thousand NGOs in India engaged in rural development, 550 in Bangladesh, and over 200 in Zimbabwe. In Kenya the number of NGOs active in development doubled from 70 in 1970 to 140 by 1980, with a further increase to some 250 by the late 1980s; the number would expand to many thousands if local women's and other grass-roots organisations were included.

This rapid growth has been spurred by the more positive attitude on the part of donors and many host governments towards the NGO sector, and by the increased availability of funds from foreign donors, both NGOs and governments. It has also been facilitated by the retreat of government provision in many developing countries, manifest in a much reduced role in welfare services as a result of public expenditure cutbacks and a weakening of its legitimacy in the face of pressures for democratisaton, which have in turn widened the potential for non-state initiatives (Robinson, 1995).

Some southern NGOs now reach very large numbers of poor people: the Grameen Bank in Bangladesh has over 160,000 borrowers, the Working Women's Forum of Madras 38,000 members, and the Self-Employed Women's Association in Ahmedabad 15,000 members (Tendler, 1987: 6). It has been estimated that in the early 1980s NGO activities reached some 100 million people in developing countries: 60 million in Asia, 25 million in Latin America, but only 12 million in Africa, although, with a rapid expansion in NGOs in the 1980s, this figure has probably increased dramatically (Schneider, 1988). By then (and if it were assumed that NGOs work primarily with the poor), NGOs would have reached approximately one in eight of those living in poverty in developing countries. More recently the 1993 *Human Development Report* judged that some 250 million people were being touched by NGOs and that the numbers would rise considerably in the years ahead (UNDP, 1993: 93).

Southern NGOs vary enormously in their approach and orientation, in their size and location of operation, in the physical, financial, and technical resources they have available, in the scale of their interventions, in the degree of support they receive from government, and, last but by no means least, in the socio-political context in which their interventions are located. They range from small localised NGOs working in a handful of villages in a single locality, to large NGOs working at a regional or national level, for the most part with funds from external sources. In addition to these local NGOs, there are also large international NGOs (often working with local representation) providing funding and support to indigenous NGOs.

A typical southern NGO is a small agency with a handful of staff working in a cluster of villages in a particular locality. Relatively few NGOs possess the staff or financial resources to work intensively at regional or national level, although it is these organisations which are the best known in government and donor circles. Most of these NGOs are engaged in promoting self-help activities, service provision, community organisation, and poverty alleviation with funding from foreign NGOs and, in some cases, government sources. In vulnerable areas, it is still far from rare for development projects to be interrupted by the need to address emergency problems, at times resulting in emergency and development programmes running alongside each other.

A common characteristic of most NGO interventions is working through groups, although some interventions, most notably emergency-type projects, work with the poor on a one-to-one basis. NGO groups range from informal community-based organisations to formal membership bodies established, for instance, for the purpose of the project, often facilitating credit or service schemes provided by the government, or else initiated by the NGOs themselves. They are bound together by voluntary contributions of time and resources and function for mutual benefit. These traits distinguish them from NGOs which act as service providers or facilitators (Fowler, 1988: 3-5; Verhagen, 1987: 21-4). In Africa these organisations 'draw cohesion and legitimacy by building on existing forms of social organisation and adapting their procedures to traditional norms of reciprocity' Bratton, 1990: 92). In Latin America, and more recently in parts of Asia, it is common for NGOs to promote and work with grass-roots organisations in order to create popular movements which can use their growing power to attempt to modify government legislation in the interests of the poor, and to strengthen democratic participation in the wider society (Korten, 1990a: 123-8; Clark, 1991; Stephen, 1990; Carroll, 1992; Bebbingron and Kopp, 1995).

There are other differences between NGO approaches, notably between the approaches frequently used in Africa and Asia, reflecting differing historical traditions and political environments. In Bangladesh, NGOs pursue remarkably similar approaches to poverty alleviation, centred on the setting up of savings and credit groups which provide the focal point not only for revolving loan schemes, but also for a range of other sectoral activities in the fields of health, education, income generation, social forestry, irrigation, etc. In this they are strongly influenced by the models promoted by the Bangladesh Rural Advancement Committee (BRAC) and the Grameen Bank.

Yet Indian NGOs generally exhibit a greater diversity of approach. Two main approaches prevail: small-scale integrated rural development on the one hand and social action on the other. The former is premissed on support for specific programmes and projects organised sectorally and implemented through grass-roots organisations (known as *sangams* in southern India). In contrast, social action groups concentrate on mobilising the poor to demand better services from government, and work for improved working conditions, higher wages, tenurial reform, etc. while the approaches are very different, there has been some convergence in recent years, with the growing belief among some NGOs that material improvements and empowerment are complementary and can reinforce each other.

In many countries in Africa, the churches play a major role in NGO development activities, many having shifted from relief to development work in the past 10 to 15 years. For instance, in Uganda most dioceses have development arms responsible for channelling funds from northern churches and NGOs to grass-roots organisations in rural areas. Similarly, foreign NGOs tend to be operational more in Africa than in Asia, in part because of the relative weakness of indigenous NGOs and the lack of suitably qualified personnel, and in part because of the many areas which government services simply do not reach and where, as a result, any intervention tends to be relatively expensive.

Trends in NGO Activities

Health care and education were prominent among the initial concerns of many NGOs in the 1950s and 1960s. Increasingly, however, NGOs have moved into projects directly targeted at alleviating poverty and attempting to raise the incomes of the poor. Thus, projects aimed at increasing poor farmers' incomes became fashionable in the 1970s, manifest in a growing concern with income generation, the supply of credit, and crop production. These were often accompanied by measures designed to improve the rural infrastructure in the shape of minor irrigation schemes, the construction of schools and community buildings, local roads, etc.

A rather different trend also emerged in the 1970s, where the emphasis was not so much on service delivery or development programmes, but on organising the poor with a view to enabling them to exercise greater influence over decisions affecting their lives. This 'empowerment' approach has its roots in the view that literacy can often become a means by which the poor can reflect on the causes of their poverty and find ways of tackling them, usually by forming activist groups which put pressure on governments to reassess their policies or persuade the rich to redistribute power and resources in favour of the poor.

New concerns came to the fore in the 1980s, such as gender and the environment, with social forestry and soil conservation prominent among environmental concerns. These reflect an increasing concern about how projects affect the wider setting in which the poor live. Part of the reason for this extension of interests comes from another characteristic which NGOs emphasise: innovation. NGOs pride themselves on being innovative, in the sense of introducing new techniques as well as in fostering novel forms of social organisation. As regards the former this has centred on the development of appropriate, low-cost, technologies, which are accessible to the poor. Similarly, as noted above, some NGOs claim to be innovative in their organisational approach, by promoting participation and forging new co-operative alliances among the poor through the formation of grass-roots organisations.

The 1990s have witnessed yet more changes in the nature of NGO activities. Work in the areas of gender and the environment has been widened, deepened, and in many ways integrated under the umbrella of 'sustainable development'. Additionally, some NGOs have focused their efforts in initiatives aimed at strengthening the power and influence of different (poorer) groups in civil society and in a range of projects and programmes striving to build up the capacity of local organisations.

Cutting across these concerns has been a growing interest in sustainability. There are two reasons for this. One stems from a concern with cost recovery, and the desire among NGOs (especially northern NGOs) to transfer the recurrent costs of project management to the community following the withdrawal of the support agency. This is based on the belief that development interventions can be sustained over the longer term only if the community assumes ownership of the project or programme. A second reason for the interest in sustainability is bound up with the desire to avoid promoting dependence on an external agency. This is based in part on NGOs' not wishing to be perceived as benevolent patrons, especially when external dependence simply replaces the influence of locally dominant elites without addressing the structural reasons for such dominance.

NGO Comparative Advantage: Assumptions and Evidence

So much for the development of the different characteristics and modes of operation of both northern and southern NGOs. In this section we focus more specifically on the advantages which NGOs are said to bring to bear on the issue of trying to solve the basic problems of development and poverty. At one time, there was widespread scepticism outside NGO circles about the potential of NGOs in development. This has now diminished, although as Cernea (1988: 17) notes, 'there are many contradictory views about the comparative advantages and weaknesses of NGOs. These views range from quasi-denial of NGO effectiveness to hyperbolic exaggeration.'

It is common (and understandable) that northern NGOs tend to project a positive image of their work and the projects that they support in developing countries. This is partly because the public has high expectations of what they can achieve, fuelled by media attention in the 1980s. As Clark astutely observes (1991: 51): 'The media project Northern NGOs as virtuous Davids fighting the Goliaths of famine, climate, government inequity, slavery and oppression. Their staff make such great sacrifices . . . their projects allow crops to grow abundantly where previously there was desert.' It is also in part a function of the literature produced by the NGOs themselves, especially that which is directed to fund-raising. There is a pervasive belief among NGOs in the superior quality of their interventions compared with those supported and executed by official donors and governments. But, to quote Clark again (1991: 53):

> there is surprisingly little objective reporting of NGO projects. Northern NGOs' own writing generally concentres on the success stories and, being aimed largely at their supporting publics, serve a propaganda purpose . . . Most contributors have an implicit faith in the 'NGO approach' which they don't want rocked. After all, one doesn't scrutinise magic too closely, otherwise it loses its charm.

One way of assessing the impact and effectiveness of NGO interventions is to attempt to isolate those features of NGOs which, it is argued, place them in a comparatively advantageous position to work with and assist the poor. In an important early analysis, Tendler (1982: 2 ff.) lists some seven 'articles of faith' about the positive nature of private voluntary organisations. These include:

- that PVOs succeed in reaching the poor;
- that the poor participate in their projects;
- that emphasis is laid more on the process through which people learn to gain control over their lives rather than in the execution of particular tasks;
- that interventions are characterised by flexibility and experimentation in large measure because they tend to be small-scale;

- and that the costs of intervention tend to be lower than more traditional official agency as well as host government interventions.

A similar sort of listing of NGO attributes is given by van der Heijden (1986: 6-7), who argues that the unique features of NGOs, or their 'comparative advantages', are:

> their ability to deliver emergency relief or development services at low cost, to many people, in remote areas; their rapid, innovative and flexible responses to emerging financial and technical assistance needs at the grass roots level; their long-standing familiarity with social sector development and poverty alleviation; their experience with small-scale development projects as well as with those requiring a high degree of involvement by, and familiarity with, the concerned target groups.

These attributes have been confirmed in some of the more recent literature which continues to make similar claims about the role and often the uniqueness of NGOs. Thus, from the World Bank, Williams (1990: 32) writes that 'international NGO have been effective in their ability to work at the grassroots level, and to operate in remote areas or those sectors that did not have efficient development activity'.

Not surprisingly, given their growing involvement in the funding of NGOs, official aid donors have tended to confirm the claims made by the NGOs themselves. Thus, according to a review of NGO projects supported by official aid agencies, Cameron and Cocking state that Canadian NGOs meet their project objectives; Danish NGOs are believed to supplement and complement official aid work; Irish NGOs are effective in meeting their objectives; British NGOs effectively complement official aid; and New Zealand NGOs contribute to the alleviation of poverty in the poorer regions of the world (1991: 18-19). And in the words of a recent overview of NGOs, undertaken by the OECD (1988: 114-15): 'In general, evaluations conducted so far by the official aid agencies of DAC members, many of them relating to rural development and social services, conclude that NGOs have a good record in rural development.' Such a view is likely to have been strongly influenced by a 1986 Canadian International Development Agency study, based on a review of 420 projects sponsored by CIDA and Canadian NGOs. This concluded not only that the vast majority of such interventions were very successful, but that a full one-third of projects appeared to have achieved financial autonomy. Overall, it is argued that the projects showed a strong rural emphasis and a 'clear focus on the poor' (OECD, 1988: 103).

This viewpoint has, however, been increasingly challenged. Indeed, more common are contributions which refine these rather bold assertions, which challenge outright one or more elements of the conventional wisdom, or which highlight what are seen as weaknesses in NGO interventions. These writings are based on a mix of personal experience, surveys of already completed evaluations, and the results of specially commissioned assessments of particular interventions in one or more countries. Among the most serious problems pinpointed are that the management of projects tends to be weak and, in part relatedly, that sustainability is very difficult to achieve (Brown and Korten, 1989). A third problem is that there is little sign of replicability of particular interventions either by the same or by other NGOs.

This clearly weakens the overall impact of NGO intervention. A typical critical assessment of the sustainability problem would be the following comment by USAID quoted by Dichter (1988: 1): 'A review of ongoing and completed AID projects in small-scale enterprise credit indicates that most never become self-sustaining even in their pure credit functions. Even more rarely does any project totally cover the costs of its non-financial components.' Indeed, detailed studies tend to suggest that NGO projects invariably founder once outside support is terminated (Cernea, 1988: 19), unless inputs are locally available, beneficiaries are strongly motivated, and the project is compatible smith existing social and economic structures (de Crombrugghe *et al.,* 1985).

On the management issue, Korten (1990a: 12) reflects an increasingly shared view that NGOs are 'characteristically weak on management and planning'. To which Clark adds (1991: 66):

> NGOs are prone to slow response resulting from cumbersome decision making, are susceptible to paralysis arising from power struggles between competing factions, and can evolve conflicting aims as different departments perceive a freedom to interpret their own role without reference to a strongly defined overall mission.

Similarly on the government/NGO contrast, with experience in East Africa, Fowler (1988) maintains that NGOs do not possess an innate comparative advantage over government institutions: rather, they have a potential comparative advantage which can be realised only if they consciously adopt management tools that are appropriate to small-scale development projects in an uncertain external environment.

In some cases, however, it is apparent that management *per se* is sometimes not such a problem, but that, especially in smaller projects, leadership can often be crucial to NGO impact. Indeed, a new article of faith is simply that 'good leadership is essential to project success' (Commonwealth Secretariat, 1987: 10). Conyers and Kaul (1990: 131) even go so far as to maintain that 'local leadership is one of the most important factors contributing to the success of most of the development projects'. Such a view has been confirmed by Tendler who, writing in 1987, drew attention to the significance of charismatic leadership in successful projects, noting that good political connections and a technocratic outlook were instrumental in their success (1987: 21-2). More detailed analysis also suggests that organisations can stagnate when leaders are away for long periods, that they are prone to decay, and that they have little potential for replication and limited capacity for absorbing new ideas. These observations lead Clark to conclude (1991: 66): 'Though leadership is critical to the success of NGOs usually little attention is paid to the development of leadership potential or to management training. And, once in post, leadership skills are rarely fostered because most NGOs are poor at delegation.'

Management and leadership questions lead naturally to the competence of NGO staff to undertake and execute projects and programmes. Although the issue does not feature widely in the published literature, it has been raised in particular by those with experience in the field. Thus Edwards (1989) maintains that he knows of no project in Zambia or Malawi in which inadequate training did not feature as a problem in project implementation. Highly committed staff are seen as an important element in NGO comparative advantage, although it is also recognised that this may create inflexibility and resistance to new ideas (Clark, 1991: 62).

Moving to the issue of replication, Brodhead and Herbert-Copley (1988: 110) argue that this is the key factor in evaluating success, but that 'the available evidence suggests that NGOs have had at best limited success in ensuring the replication of their work'. For Tendler (1987: v), there is an inherent conflict between small scale and replicability: smallness and social homogeneity often get lost when NGOs expand. She also links the issue of replicability to the leadership question, arguing that, unless the project is replicated by its founder, the chances of success in replication are thin (ibid: 21). Similarly, Cernea (1988: 18) argues that staff intensity and motivation are essential to successful replication. While one component of the literature highlights these weaknesses of NGO intervention, another goes on to challenge some other articles of faith.

Thus, Annis comments (1987: 129): 'In the face of pervasive poverty, for example, "small-scale" can merely be "insignificant"—"Politically-independent" can mean "powerless" or "disconnected"—"Low-cost" can mean "underfinanced" or "poor quality"—And 'innovative' can mean simply "temporary" or "unsustainable."' What is more, Tendler (1982) contends that in practice many NGO interventions do not reach the lowest 40 per cent of the poor, and that they are neither participatory nor low-cost, although she goes on to argue that projects are not necessarily failures as a result of being burdened with these particular characteristics.

Similarly, from a study of NGO projects in two villages in the Indian state of Gujarat, Griffiths (1987: 43) concludes that, despite a systematic attempt at proper identification and targeting, 'the poorest were by and large not identified whatever the circumstances'. Nevertheless, in contrast, Avina (1990) reports that, in his experience, the beneficiaries are among the poorest sectors of society, even if some of the not-so-poor also benefit. On the cost issue, a series of USAID-sponsored studies on the effectiveness of NGO projects in health, nutrition, water supply, and sanitation, found that the largely voluntary nature of NGO activities, their commitment to use low cost technologies and streamlined services, and low staff costs, enable them to operate efficiently on low budgets' (Cernea, 1988: 18). In contrast, Bowden (1990) maintains that NGO interventions are not low-cost, Brodhead and Herbert-Copley (1988: 100) that low cost is no guarantee of cost-effectiveness, and Korten (1990*a* 12) that the projects are not is cost-effective as the NGOs themselves think. Brodhead hints at an underlying tension between simultaneously achieving the twin goals of reaching the poorest and executing low-cost projects.

He draws on work by Chambers (1983) to suggest that projects which effectively reach the poor require a high degree of administrative skill and capability, which means higher costs per beneficiary. On the question of the innovative nature of NGO activities, Kottack's analysis leads him to conclude that the projects promoted are anything but innovatory (1985: 323). In contrast, USAID (19S6) asserts that NGOs are adaptive and innovative in their approach.

As Tendler is often seen as a critic of the conventional wisdom, her contrasting views on innovation are particularly noteworthy. In 1982 (1982: 114), she wrote that PVOs seem to be exceptionally innovative in relation to credit to small business, but five years later she maintained (1987: vi) that NGOs often claim they are pioneering a new approach when they are merely reinventing the wheel. There has been considerable discussion in the literature on the issue of participation and its importance to project impact. The assumption, as Brodhead and Herbert-Copley (1988: 123) point out, is that participation increases the likelihood of attaining the project's objectives and its sustainability, as well as promoting a more equal distribution of project benefits.

Their own view is that participation is important but by no means a sufficient condition for project success. This contrasts with the 1986 CIDA study which argued that community participation was one of three factors leading to project success. In strong contrast, Tendler (1982, 1987) maintains that projects which are not participatory but which are top-down and authoritarian can be very successful. Similarly, de Crombrugghe *et al.* (1985: 80) argue that projects may sometimes succeed without the beneficiaries being involved in the identification of needs, even if their evidence also leads them to the view that projects 'almost always fail' if the beneficiaries are excluded in the planning phase. Moving from the particular to the general issue of the overall impact of NGO interventions, what is noteworthy is that, with only rare exceptions, most substantive analyses based on commissioned studies come to fairly gloomy conclusions about the performance of NGO projects, even though there is considerable reluctance on the part of analysts to be drawn into making overall or general statements about impact— even in cases where opinions are based on the examination of only a limited number of interventions.

The main reasons put forward for this high degree of diffidence are: the lack of data with which assessments can confidently be made, the differing quality of evaluations which have found their way into the public domain, and a reluctance to make broader generalisations from limited evidence. These points are made strongly, for instance, in the writings of Brodhead and Herbert-Copley (1988) and de Crombrugghe *et al.* (1985). A typical comment reflecting this sense of unease would be the following (Smith quoted in Gorman, 1984: 146, 155): 'the unevenness of evaluations of pvo projects does not help to prove pvo claims that they are more effective than governmental agencies in certain areas of development. . . there is insufficient evidence to substantiate these claims solidly . . . The rhetoric is at times great but adequate information is sparse.'

In spite of the reservations, some overall judgements have been made. They usually share the viewpoint that, while the projects selected are frequently those which the NGOs themselves believe are among their better ones, independent assessments frequently come to far less favourable judgements about performance and impact. Not surprisingly, therefore, the overall view of the impact of NGOs in poverty-alleviating and/or income-generating projects is one ranging from, say, mediocre to poor, rather than, say, from acceptable to good. These and similar comments from this critical school lead on to the highlighting of a fourth problem, which, it is argued, plays a major contributory role in the low success rate of their projects. This is the vagueness of many of the objectives of projects, leading to the charge that imprecise objectives are bound to be difficult to monitor and evaluate. In this vein, de Crombrugghe *et al.* argued in the mid-1980s that steps needed to be taken to improve the way that projects were identified, prepared, and initially appraised (1985: 36). Nevertheless, towards the end of the decade, there was still 'a widespread need for better project planning' (OECD, 1988: 115).

A number of more recent studies have placed increased emphasis on yet more factors said to influence project performance. Particular emphasis is placed on the importance of the wider environment—the large number of factors external to the project—which, it is argued, not only need to be analysed when initiating and executing particular projects, but which also help to explain what appears to be the relatively poor-performance of NGO projects. For instance, Tendler (1987: 102) maintains that the success of NGO operations depends upon a complex set of factors including macroeconomic and socio-political environmental factors, many of which are otters beyond the control of the NGOs.

Similarly, Carr *et al.* (1984: 1) contend that a *sine qua non* of any evaluation of performance is a full understanding of the environment in which the project is located; only when this is achieved can one begin to understand the changes which are talking place, and among them the ones which are applicable to project intervention. More dynamic and historical factors are also highlighted. Thus, Brown (1990) and Korten (1990b) write about the role and importance of institutions and organisations for achieving sustainable development, and draw on an even wider literature to illustrate their concerns in these areas.

A discussion of the importance of power, power relations, and empowerment processes in understanding current impact and future prospects is also relevant in this context. Debate on these issues can be highly specific, relating to elites and interest-group interests that directly impinge upon the project, or it can be very broad and general, focusing on the nature of the state and the manner in which it is possible for agents external to central power structures to meet the objectives of their very different agendas. Usually, however, when discussion of impact takes place within these wider parameters it also tends to veer towards pessimism.

When discussion is broadened to external factors it usually emphasises the complexity of factors affecting project performance. Some authors have argued that, because the communities with which NGOs work are always changing, if not the objectives then at least the means to achieve these objectives need continually to be re-assessed and altered as circumstances, both internal and external to the project, change. Conyers and Kaul (1990: 132) suggest that this inevitably brings conflict. Yet another layer of complexity is added when it is argued that project success in one time-period could well be the cause of problems in another. This is well illustrated by a recent review of a World Lutheran Federation water project in West Nile Uganda, where clear success in easing the plight of thousands of people whose lives were threatened, contributed to the build-up of future problems.

This chapter suggests chat it is by no means easy to come

to any firm overall conclusions about either the factors which characterise the uniqueness of NGO interventions or the degree to which NGOs have succeeded in their task of helping to alleviate poverty. It is clearly far from simple to judge whether the views of the optimists or the pessimists better reflect reality. There are four main reasons for this. The first is simply a lack of data. For all the claims and counter-claims made and for all the evidence provided, the extent of reliable evidence upon which judgements have been and are made still remains minute in comparison with both the absolute numbers of NGO interventions and the very different types of project embarked upon. The second is that there still seems to be confusion in the eyes of both the general public and the agencies over claims and assertions about the comparative advantage of NGOs and the evidence which is available. The third is the growing realisation that a range of both complex and external factors play a powerful role in influencing the outcome of NGO intervention in very different social, economic, and political contexts.

Finally, judging impact is handicapped by the lack of an agreed method of assessing the performance of NGO protects and programmes. It is to the question of impact assessment that we now turn: the next chapter examines the problems underlying the evaluation of NGO project performance and existing approaches to NGO evaluation, and ends by setting out the approach used in the case-studies contained in this book.

REFERENCES

Lowry, Richie P., 1974, *Social Problems:* A Critical Analysis of Theories and Public Policy, Lexington, Mass.: D.C. Heath.

Rosenberg, Bernard, Israel Gerver, and F. William Howton, 1971, *Mass Society in Crisis: Social Problems and Social Pathology.* 2nd ed, New York: Macmillan, 1st edition. 1964.

CHAPTER 6

Evolving Accountability of Voluntary Organisations

> Anyone who can walk to the welfare office can walk to work.
>
> —*Al Capp*

The praxis of accountability has become contentious because quite unlike the early social reformers, the church-based or Gandhian institutions, even some of the efforts initiated by the political parties, the modern NGO phenomenon (at least a significant section of it) locates itself in an explicit critique of the state and political parties, particularly their relative inability to respond meaningfully to the survival and dignity issues of the poor and the excluded. This is even more true of support NGOs (middle class and mainly urban) who seek to work, not directly with base communities, but field organisations involved in an effort to improve their efficacy, individually and collectively.

Much of this orientation evolved in a phase when donor organisations, official or otherwise, national or foreign, started stressing the inefficacy of working through official structures to tackle widespread but local issues of oppression and survival. From the formal recognition granted to NGOs in the Seventh Eve Year Plan to the shift in the priorities of multilateral, bilateral and private co-financing agencies, the period from the late 1970s has witnessed a massive escalation of both support and funding to NGO formations.

Not unexpectedly, this change in environment led to a major explosion in the number of NGOs. While a large part of this munificence was channelised towards conventional charity and developmental organisations, a large residual market was simultaneously created for NGOs working with a political orientation. Thus new groups, whether working directly with the concerned populace in the field, or as support organisations mediating between micro social action groups, or between them and the state, through a diverse set of activities earlier unknown in the NGO world, acquired a new presence.

Through seminars and workshops, theatre and films, newsletters and journals, lobbying and networking, these new groupings with specialised skills attempted to reach out to both the grassroots and the policy-makers. Central to this new enterprise were new ideological debates — on human rights, ecology, feminism and the law — efforts at reconstituting the epistemological universe in which meanings are ascribed to political and developmental activity. At one level, this proliferation and diversity in the NGO sector and discourse about it has contributed to the difficulty in making sense of this activity. Second, the stakes of the game have become considerably higher, given particularly the centrality of the NGOs in development policy formulation and practice. Finally, with grassroots and social movement studies more focused on NGO activism than political parries and movements or organisations of workers and peasants, we have the emergence of a new academic market with considerable funding support. One interesting implication of all this has been the progressive radicalisation of language and concepts. The shift from the mid- 1970s towards NGOs as a favoured entity for funding support owes much to their 'brand distinction' from official agencies. In relative terms, they were seen as locally rooted and environmentally sensitive, flexible, low-cost and honest, and thus 'proper' instruments to reach the people. However, as criticism grew of top-down, non-participative approaches to development and democracy, much greater stress began to be laid on processes rather than products, particularly those that helped in the conscientisation, mobilisation and organisation of the poor and hitherto excluded.

This heightened radicalism led to a purposive devaluation of the notion of service, of doing good, of helping others in need. Older voluntary formations, albeit of a conventional charity and development type, were made to appear as irrelevant. It also led to a decline in the importance of material interventions in the lives of the poor, since activities like introducing new technologies, focussing on income generation through production, etc., were construed as consolidating the capitalist system, as helping the better-off. Activities and organisations were now sought to be judged with respect to their 'political' potential and role.

The assumption of this new political role, accompanied by radical rhetoric, has generated new pressures from diverse sources on the NGO sector. As a result of the new expectations that NGOs have generated, there is an overloading of demands from the ground. Networking and coordination, combined with servicing grassroots groups and struggles, is a complex task. The inability to satisfy these expectations has led to the trading of vilificatory charges—that NGOs have become corrupt, lazy, used to an easy lifestyle, distanced from base communities and groups—some of it unfortunately true. The 'phobia' about the sector emerging as the new dissenting force (a result both of description and self-description) has led to a new alliance of forces arraigned against the sector as also new, official, restrictive conditionalities.

As we move towards the end of the millennium, the country faces a daunting situation. More than seven years of attempts at economic liberalisation, designed more to globally integrate the economy and roll back the State even from its constitutionally mandated role rather than 'free' domestic production and distribution, has created a new stratum of the relatively deprived. Whatever be one's personal assessment of the reform initiatives, it is difficult to deny the increase in inequality, and this when the masses remain deprived of the basic requirements of a life with dignity. Our formal political structure is in shambles, unable not just to enable stable rule but even to intervene positively in daily life. Many of the protective legislations have been watered down. Above all, akin to the situation of the late 1960s and 1970s, the State and its agencies are once again being viewed with distrust.

The Challenges Ahead

The debate about NGOs and community initiatives and formations thus needs to be located in this context. Issues of accountability and modes to ensure that the NGOs remain transparent have to be tackled with urgency if we are to re-infuse the sector with a new spirit. Otherwise, notwithstanding greater funding support and glamour, the inflow of dedicated and creative people, particularly the young, is likely to dry up.

This needs a little elaboration. A quarter century back, the epistemic shift in the voluntary sector was from service to empowerment, development to political action. The drawing edge came from ideological commitment. NGOs, whatever their organisational affiliation —Gandhian, religious or Marxist/ Socialist—seemed keen to focus on the poor. As NGOs started offering a viable career option, the social base of their cadres slowly started changing. Given the new activity mix, more so of the intermediary support organisations, the emphasis shifted to skill and efficacy. My argument is not that the new generation of NGO activists is less concerned about issues related to the poor and deprived. It is that they are, in relative terms, more concerned about themselves and thus relate differently to issues of accountability to their respective organisations as also to the people they work for and with.

I began this brief note with SWRC Tilonia and Bunker Boy who began his 'developmental career' in the early 1970s. Let me end with another tale. A few months back, Sanjoy Ghose, secretary of the Association of Voluntary Agencies for Rural Development-North East (AVARD-NE) was abducted and killed by the United Liberation Front of Assam (ULFA). Sanjoy and his associates had for the past few years been working in Majuli island in the Brahmaputra in Assam.

Every year, the island suffered massive erosion, particularly when the river was in spate. Huge sums of money were doled out to local contractors to shore up the banks. AVARD-NE started organising the local people to bid for the contract such that the anti-erosion work could be carried out at a much lower cost. Evidently, this displeased the local contractors as also the ULFA which received 'protection money from the contractors.

Sanjoy and his associates were warned and asked to vacate the island. They too organised public meetings and sought guidance from the people as to whether they should stay and continue work or leave. The people supported them. The result: Sanjoy was abducted and 'eliminated'. This happened to a well-connected, high-profile worker. The situation of less well-placed activists working in hostile contexts can be well imagined.

How should NGO groups and activists work in such hostile contexts? Who are they accountable to? Caught often between the conflicting demands placed on them by the state and the 'militants' merely having the goodwill and support of the people is unlikely to be sufficient to ensure their security and survival. Such a situation is by no means rare. Not just the North East or Kashmir, but large pockets in Bihar, Orissa, Madhya Pradesh, Andhra Pradesh and Maharashtra are today marked by serious unrest and the presence of armed militant groups. Often times, these militant groups demand not just 'protection' money from organisations working in their zones of influence, but seek to alter the objectives of the organisation. Most groups either acquiesce to the demands or withdraw from the area. What then about the people to whom too the NGO owes commitment?

There are no easy answers to such dilemmas. Without for a moment downplaying the risks associated with working in such situations, the only option available to the NGO is to rely on the collective goodwill and strength of the people who remain the final *raison d'etre* of its existence. Sometimes the price paid is high, as in the case of Sanjoy. Reportedly, the residents of Majuli island have resolved to continue the good work initiated by AVARD-NE. *And* this is no small victory.

REFERENCES

Bernard, Jessie, 1957, *Social Problems at Midcentury: Role, Status and Stress in a Context of Abundance,* New York: Holt, Rinehart and Winston.

Coser, Lewis, A., 1956, *The Functions of Social Conflict,* New York: The Free Press.

Currie, Eliott, and Jerome H. Skolnick, 1984, *America's Problem* Boston: Little Brown and Company.

Habennas, Jurgen, 1971, *Toward a Rational Society,* London:" Heinemann.

Hawkesworth, M.E., 1988, *Theoretical Issues in Policy Analysis 'New* York: State University of the New York Press.

Heworth, L, 1960, "The Experimenting Society: Devey and Jorden", *Ethics,* 71: 27-40.

Healy, Paul, 1986, "Interpretive Policy Inquiry: A Response to the Limitations of the Received View", *Policy Sciences,* 19: 381-396.

Myrdal, Gunnar, 1968, *Asian Drama: An Inquiry into the Poverty of Nations,* Harmondsworth: Fenguin, 3 Vols.

New house, J.P., 1974, *The Health Insurance Study-A Summary, Santa* Monica, California: Rand.

Rubington, Earl, and Martin S. Weinberg, eds., 1977, *The Study of Social Problems: Five Perspectives,* New York: Oxford University Press.

Shaw, Clifford, Henry Mckay, et al., 1929, *Delinquency Areas: A Study of the Geographical Distribution of School Truants, Juvenile Delinquents and Adult Offenders in Chicago,* Chicago: University of Chicago press.

Shaw, Clifford, and Henry Mckay, *1942, Juvenile Delinquency and Urban Areas,* Chicago: University of Chicago Press.

Smith, Adam, 1948, *Moral and Political Philosophy,* H.W. Schneider, ed. New York: American Book Company.

CHAPTER 7

Contribution of NGOs to Development

> A liberty subject to law and subordinate to the common welfare.
>
> —*Bainbridge Colby*

After the first three decades of planning for development by the government, there was a widespread realisation that the government systems were too rigid and standardised to evolve plans that would meet the varied requirements of this vast country. The government's implementing instrument, the bureaucracy, was too self-centred to attend to people's needs. Both the higher echelons of government and the observers of ground reality felt that government in India was emerging as monolithic, inefficient, highly bureaucratic and corrupt. A new approach and style of working seemed necessary to help in evolving programmes and implementing them in a participatory manner to meet the requirements of the local people with more accountability and transparency, and better quality of development and service delivery. Though the government was committed to people's participation from the beginning of planning in India, such participation had remained confined only to rhetoric; the system had no clue what it meant in practice. Finding that community development was not working as intended, in the early 1960s, the country adopted the model of Panchayati Raj, as if self-government would automatically make development people-oriented. This did not happen. Beginning in the 1970s, and more so in the

1980s, many development NGOs came on the scene; they were distinct, on the one hand, from the government agencies and, on the other, from philanthropic organisations.

By 1997, about 14,000 NGOs were registered with the Home Ministry under the Foreign Currency Regulation Act (FCRA) and many more were registered as societies under the Societies Registration Act, 1860. The development NGOs appear to have made some impact. The government as well as other funding organisations have begun to insist on the involvement of NGOs in planning and implementing the development projects and programmes. It is obvious, however, that even thousands of NGOs cannot replace the role of the government. What role and contribution should then be expected of the development NGOs? How do they influence the development scenario beyond the areas they serve? This chapter attempts to explore some of these issues. Its findings are based largely on the personal experiences and understanding of the authors of working of the NGOs. The chapter also presents a short case study of an NGO which has achieved notable success in implementing a participatory watershed development project funded by the Government of India in about 35 villages in Savarkundla *taluka,* of Bhavnagar district, Gujarat.

NGOs' Contribution Issues

The achievements of a development NGO, namely, the Aga Khan Rural Support Programme (AKRSP), working in three districts in Gujarat since 1984, on selected programmes and the reported performance of government agencies.

The achievements of the NGO are by no means negligible, but juxtaposed against the work done by government agencies, they pale into insignificance. What then is the import of the AKRSP's contribution or of similar NGOs, whose work looks small when compared to that done by the government agencies? This question cropped up in 1985 when the AKRSP had completed a lift irrigation project an,d built a percolation tank in a very short time with actual cost being less than that estimated by the government. The quality of work looked very impressive, and in fact, has continued to remain so all these years. When the NGO was asked about the special value of the structures, it proudly pointed to the quality and cost-effectiveness. Government could not have done it through its run of contractors. A well-wisher of the NGO sector asked, 'Are you then a good contractor for the government?'

'Certainly not; our motive was not profit. It was good work for the benefit of the people', was the pet reply. Not fully satisfied, the well-wisher asked, 'Are you then a contractor for the people?' The response was that the AKRSP was a people's supporter. It raised a very relevant question: What is the role of an NGO in a programme which the government has been implementing for decades? It was obvious that, even after expansion in the not so distant future, the AKRSP was no match for the magnitude of the government's programme. It was then realised that the contribution of development NGOs such as the AKRSP should be judged not in quantitative but in qualitative terms. However, in order to judge the quality, some standard and comparable parameters have to be evolved. In projects and programmes that have to be implemented with active community/people's participation, the following parameters may be considered:

- People's participation;
- technical excellence;
- cost-effectiveness;
- equity-concern for the deprived, and for women;
- institutional, financial, and environmental sustainability;
- accountability/transparency.

The AKRSP has always strived to achieve these quality parameters in its programmes. None of its percolation tanks or check dams has burst. Utilisation of the potential of the canals, in which people have taken over the management under the guidance of the AKRSP, is dose to 80 per cent and recovery of water charges is almost 100 per cent. Survival rate of its saplings and plantations is over 70 per cent, and more than 85 per cent of the biogas plants are working satisfactorily. The strength of the development NGOs, therefore, lies in the qualitative aspects of their work. There has been a conscious effort on the part of the NGOs to ensure quality, cost-effectiveness, and accountability in whatever they try to do.

The mission statement of another NGO, the Development Support Centre (DSC), says:

> Development Support Centre is established to provide support to people-centred organisations, programmes and policies in natural resource development with an emphasis on participation, equity, efficiency, cost effectiveness, honesty and transparency.

However, even if the performance of NGOs is good compared with that of projects and programmes implemented by the government agencies, a question may be asked, 'So what?' If the government remains a much larger actor in the development programmes, what exactly is the value of NGOs' contribution? Is it limited to the villages they work in? The AKRSP, for instance, hardly works in more than two per cent of the villages in Gujarat. Fortunately, the efforts of development NGOs to improve the quality of programmes do not remain limited to the villages or the areas where they work; there are also a lot of spread effects. Let us examine a few of them.

Pressurising the Government to Improve Performance

People in villages served by NGOs start comparing similar work done by government agencies and then demand an improvement in quality. For instance, village leaders of Dhandhalpur in Sayla *taluka* (Surendranagar district), one of the three project areas of the AKRSP, approached the district administration to improve the quality of a check dam being constructed by a contractor which was obviously inferior to the check dams constructed by the AKRSP. The government contractor had to improve his work. Thus, quality work by reputed and credible NGOs generates pressure on the government systems and some positive response from the government may follow as illustrated. The AKRSP's biogas programme in Junagadh district, the programme of Sadguru Water Development Foundation to promote lift irrigation and social forestry in Panchmahals district and artificial insemination services run by the Bharatiya Agro Industries Foundation in several districts, have the potential, by virtue of their quality, to create pressure on the government to improve its performance in the same field. With some initiative and efforts the 'islands of success could spread to a larger area' (Arya, 1996).

Institutionalising Changes in Systems and Procedures

NGOs, particularly those in the area of natural resource development, have to interact closely with government agencies to obtain official permissions at various steps and, often, funding assistance. Of the Rs 1,766 lakhs spent up to 1997, by the AKRSP on their programmes, government funding accounted for about one-third. For certain programmes, such as biogas production, the share was much higher. Close interaction with the government on financial and procedural matters often leads to appreciation by government agencies of the quality work being done by the NGOs. Thus, when they agree to provide support to NGOs, the government agencies have to modify their own systems and procedures to make them more flexible and locally relevant. Interestingly, when NGOs participate in government programmes, they bring up issues which have not been previously considered by government officials. For example, since the early 1970s, the Government of India has adopted the command area development programme which concentrates on only the on-farm development below the outlets and that too only on the sites of major and medium irrigation works. Interestingly, the issue of the inappropriateness of such a restricted approach was brought up by Anil C. Shah in the Working Group on Participatory Irrigation Management (PIM) set up by the Planning Commission for the Ninth Five Year Plan. The government was persuaded to broaden its improvement strategy to include minor irrigation works and the irrigation systems above the outlets. The AKRSP has successfully carried out the rehabilitation of structures in the minor irrigation sector. Influenced by the experiments, the Gujarat Government has already agreed to make PIM all-encompassing.

Strengthening Participation

The greatest strength of NGOs is their approach and method for enlisting people's participation. Working informally in a friendly manner, they do not undertake development as government agencies generally do, with the primary concern being the achievement of a certain target irrespective of the needs and priorities of the people. They do not confine themselves merely to consultation as government agencies sometimes do, but they work for popular participation in planning, implementation and management of local resources. The NGOs increasingly play a supportive role rather than become implementing bodies themselves. Adoption of the Participatory Rural Appraisal (PRA) technique since 1987 has proved extremely valuable for development NGOs as it helps them to go beyond the traditional leadership of the village, usually the elderly males, and reach out to ordinary women and men working on their farms or at home to learn from them about their problems and the possible solutions. PRA also helps to determine people's priorities and what responsibility they can accept if appropriate development schemes come up.

The NGOs have readily accepted the principle of people's contribution as they could recognise its value as, to use World Bank terminology, 'a litmus test' to ensure genuine participation in and acceptance of a programme. Following the efforts of Anil C. Shah the principle of contribution was incorporated in PIM in Gujarat and in the recommendations of the Working Group for the Ninth Five Year Plan, 1997-2002. When the officials of the Gujarat Land Development Corporation (a government agency), have visited the villages where NGOs have carried out watershed programmes, they have been embarrassed to learn that the government works were of poor quality, easily damaged in a short time, and not maintained by the people— because they were not works 'of the people'. On the other hand, people considered the works promoted by

NGOs as 'their own' and maintained them. Government officers visiting these programmes could not but appreciate the sustainability of programmes where people were genuinely involved in their development.

Such demonstration effect has led government agencies, particularly at the higher level in central and state governments, to appreciate the need to integrate the participatory approach in their development schemes. The work done in Ralegan Siddhi, and by MYRADA, AKRSP, and KRIBHCO has helped the Ministry of Rural Development to formulate its watershed development programme, launched in October 1994, on the participation principle. Similarly, the impact of the AKRSP's participatory canal management in Bharuch district has persuaded the Government of Gujarat to adopt participatory irrigation management. NGOs, which by and large steer clear of electoral and party politics seek to influence public policies and practices on the strength of their close collaboration with the people.

This may not be an agenda for reforming political institutions and political processes (Bhatt, 1995) but it certainly aims to reform public systems. The central element in these two approaches of seeking to influence public policy and reforming political institutions is that of appropriate and adequate assessment of ground realities and community needs.

Promoting Sustainability

Sustainability is not merely sturdy structures and their good maintenance, although these are necessary conditions for the success of development projects; they raise the production potential of factors of production. The most important aspect is the sustainability of people's institutions which are expected to create and manage schemes that are developed with substantial financial assistance from the government. NGOs have understood the sustainability aspect better and continue to spread the message through their efforts. For instance, to ensure institutional sustainability Anil C. Shah, in 1992 as chief executive of the AKRSP, persuaded the irrigation minister of the government of Gujarat that the canal irrigation cooperatives should be obliged to charge 'not less than' the government rates rather than 'not more than' the government rates. Since a good number of lift irrigation and canal schemes are managed by farmers, with NGO support, in a financially sustainable manner without government assistance for operation and maintenance (O&M), the government should be encouraged to charge water rates that cover at least O&M costs.

Thus, some NGOs support reduction of subsidies which perpetuate dependence on government. The approach to strengthening institutional sustainability, which implicitly ensures technical and financial sustainability, also strengthens environmental sustainability. Broad-based participation of the village communities helps in starting debates on the best possible use of natural resources (such as land and water) which have competing public *vs.* private, men *vs.* women, rich *vs.* poor) and alternative (domestic *vs.* irrigation) uses. The NGOs are generally in a better position to both comprehend people's perspective at the local level and share with people the changing perspective at the global level. In this sense they 'act locally and think globally'.

Collaboration between Government and NGOs

In a number of schemes, particularly those promoted by the Government of India, where cooperation and participation of people are considered essential, collaboration of NGOs is welcomed. For instance, in the area of development and management of natural resources, for such schemes as Joint Forest Management, Participatory Irrigation Management, and Watershed Development, government agencies have been seeking collaboration with NGOs. Fruitful relationships emerge when NGOs respond positively, appreciating that the government is to remain the major actor in rural development and collaborative efforts will better serve the common cause of helping the people. In the process, NGOs also get opportunities to 'upscale NGO intervention without a substantial increase in staff and operations' (Fernandez, 1996). The collaborative arrangements also help to identify issues that need to be addressed to evolve healthy and efficient working relations on various fronts. Some of these issues are listed next:

(1) To enable the NGOs to participate with ease and dignity, there is a need to simplify the government systems and procedures. This can be attempted by an NGO such as the DSC which can draw upon the experience of government systems and also has a firsthand knowledge of the special requirements of NGOs and people's organisations.

(2) NGOs have found in scheme after scheme that it is much easier to work with the Government of India than with the state governments and, similarly, with senior officers rather than with officials at the district, block and village levels, in that order. The lower level functionaries perceive NGOs as an 'encroachment on their territory (Arya, 1996). There is a need for organised fora where policy and operations issues can be brought up and resolved. State-level working groups with multi-source membership of government officers, NGOs, and academics have proved a convenient mechanism in Gujarat for programmes of PIM and JFM. Similarly, there is a need for coordination committees with multi-source membership at regional and district levels where problems of implementation can be sorted out. After a study of government/NGO collaboration in Rajasthan, it was found that 'delinked autonomous structures' are better suited to promote a healthy relationship. At the same time, depending solely on government funding creates dependency, leading to gratuitous compromises (Gulati, 1996). However, experience has also shown that merely setting up such working groups and coordination committees does not guarantee their regular and satisfactory working. Usually, NGOs have to cake the initiative to ensure their active functioning. It would be much better if a reputed NGO leader headed such fora. Such an arrangement is not uncommon

with the Government of India, although rare in the states.

(3) Government agencies collaborating with the NGOs usually expect the latter to take the responsibility of creating awareness and motivation amongst the people about development schemes. The actual implementation, they assume, should be done by the government agencies which have technical competence and their 'own' resources. However, experience has shown that just bringing people to the government agencies does not lead to participatory development. The NGOs must remain involved in implementation to ensure that people's knowledge, skills and needs are properly integrated. Knowing that there are elements of reluctance in government/NGO partnership (Ferrington and Babington, 1993), it is possible to attempt organisational designs for optimum drawing of relative strengths in this partnership. This may be termed as 'joining of strengths'. The DSC has tried to work out, for each step of planning, implementation, and management, the contribution each partner should make depending upon its relative strength. The comparative advantage of the government is large resources and spread of technical manpower, while the strength of NGOs lies in their commitment to reaching difficult areas and deprived sections. 'Joining of strengths' is more easily understood and agreed upon when both partners fully realise that their common goal is to develop the capability of the people and their institutions to take maximum responsibility for their own development, through a strong sense of 'ownership', framing of rules and enforcing discipline, transparency in operation, and sound financial management (Fernandez, 1996). However, admittedly, only development NGOs aim at such 'joining of strengths' and not the 'action NGOs', because the latter have a different and perhaps larger agenda of transforming social and political conditions in favour

of the poor (Pandey, 1991). Indeed, the action groups may, at a later date, desire to collaborate with the government, at which time the theme of 'joining of strengths' would apply.

(4) With increasing demand for contribution by NGOs in government schemes, it has been found that there is a dearth of suitable NGOs particularly in the area of natural resource development. The DSC has, therefore, taken the initiative to encourage and support new voluntary organisations and those working in traditional voluntary sectors, such as health and education, to facilitate their entry into the area of natural resource development. The emerging issue, then, is one of laying down the criteria and then activating the process of NGO selection. It has been possible to bring in several such voluntary organisations to work as implementing agencies for the watershed programme. The DSC is offering support to such new entrants to develop their capability in organisational, technical, and management areas. The DSC's experience, so far, has been that many voluntary organisations find it difficult to appreciate that natural resource management requires technical and organisational inputs which are new for them, and that participatory development demands skills different from those required for inservice delivery activities. For most of the existing voluntary organisations, it is a steep climb, requiring unloading of past baggage to become a learning organisation, readily engaging with their staff, without status barriers, into open sharing and critical reflection. Of course, there are some voluntary organisations that have developed their capability quite rapidly with support of this kind.

The five major areas identified here cover the most vital aspects related to the working of the NGOs and their immediate and larger contribution to the development process. The following section, briefly reviews the experience of an NGO which has, since October 1994, planned and implemented a land and water resource development project with people's participation. The NGO was provided technical and professional support by the DSC. Interestingly, although the NGO had had a long experience of more than 50 years, it was receptive to outside professional support and was willing to try out new approaches in planning and implementing.

CASE STUDY: KUNDLA TALUKA GRAM SEWA MANDAL (KTGSM)

The Kundla Taluka Gram Sewa Mandal (KTGSM) has its roots in Gandhian ideology. Three of the founding members of the Mandal had actively participated in the freedom struggle. Interestingly, each had his special interest in a different area and each pursued work in his respective area of interest. The economic programme of the then informal Mandal was initiated way back in 1936. However, the Mandal was formally registered as a society in 1955. Deeply influenced by the Gandhian idea of *'Gram Swaraj'*, establishment of Khadi and village industries for generating non-farm employment in villages emerged as the main programme of the Mandal. The Mandal also opened primary and secondary schools in a few villages on the lines of 'Buniyadi Talim' (basic education).

The villages in Savarkundla are inhabited mainly by patels, rajputs, kolis, ahirs, harijans, rabaris, and Muslims. The socio-economic status of patels and rajputs is generally better, and among kolis and ahirs some have been able to improve their conditions. However, kolis, ahirs, harijans, rabaris, and Muslims have remained socially backward. The *taluka* receives low and irregular rainfall ranging between 400 to 650 mm, more than 90 per cent of it during June to August. It is covered under the government's Drought Prone Areas Programme (DPAP).

There is acute water shortage both for agriculture and drinking and domestic purposes in years when rainfall is below normal. According to the 1991 Census, the percentage of irrigated to total cultivated area was 9.9 per cent, which was lower than in many other *talukas* in Bhavnagar district and also in comparison with the district and state averages of 23 and 27 per cent, respectively.

The Khadi enterprise with its headquarters in Savarkundla has a national marketing network and supports more than 2,000 families. The spindles, yarn, and other accessories are supplied through 22 sub-centres in the programme area. During the 1990s, average annual sale of Khadi has been valued at over Rs 17 million. Besides Khadi, the Mandal also manages dyeing and printing, an oil milling unit, condiment units, and manufacture of soap from inedible oils.

A residential educational centre was developed in Khadasali, a village about 25 kilometres away from Savarkundla, the *taluka* headquarters. From a very modest beginning in the late 1940s, the campus now has developed schooling facilities up to the higher secondary level. Agriculture and animal husbandry are special vocational subjects. There is a separate hostel for girls. Use of hybrid seeds, biochemical inputs, and agro-mechanical devices is taught and students and teachers carry out extension activities in the neighbouring villages.

In 1982, a cyclone struck the area and rains ravaged crops and settlements. With financial aid from OXFAM, the Mandal carried out relief operations and as a part of rehabilitation organised vegetable growing in the river bed into a co-operative. The Mandal helped in regularising the tenurial rights of the landless and small cultivators.

In 1984, the Christian Children Fund (CCF), an American donor agency, supporting the children from poor families for their total development, agreed to fund a project in the villages where the KTGSM operated. By 1997, more than 700 children from about 570 families had been provided support for schooling, better nutrition and personality development. Interestingly, the village-level workers who identify poor families and eligible children therein, have themselves benefited from the programme during their childhood. Besides supporting individual children, the programme provides for community building, such as pre-school child care arrangement (running *Balwadis),* mother and child health care clinics and support for the housing and vocational guidance of high school children.

The programme also supports creation of community assets to raise income generating capacities of poor families. Under a project taken up in the early 1990s, four check dams were constructed in a row on a small rivulet to impound rain water. Deep cuts and erosions were also plugged. The project had a very positive impact. The recharge in wells improved so much that wells which otherwise used to go dry by February had water the following summer. Encouraged by this experiment, the Mandal planned more projects under another government scheme, the Sarvodaya Yojna. In 1992-93, the Mandal supported about 50 *bandharas* (earthen bunds) in which farmers had to contribute 50 per cent of the total cost.

The *bandharas* and check dams caught the imagination of the people quickly mainly because in almost all the villages the water table had been going down rapidly. Since early 1980s, and particularly after 1987 (a year of severe drought), digging of wells and bore wells had picked up. The topography of the *taluka* is not suitable for any canal irrigation projects because the *taluka* is almost divided into two parts by a hilly ridge known as Lamdhar. Rain water runs off on both sides of the ridge and farmers rely exclusively on ground water sources for irrigation.

The Project

Encouraged by the results of *bandharas* and check dams, the KTGSM wanted to launch a similar project on a larger scale if only funds were available. It had identified the development of agriculture in the drought-prone *taluka* of Savarkundla as the key area for its intervention. Incidentally, the Department of Rural Development, Ministry of Rural Areas, Government of India, was keen to finance some innovative projects under the third stream of Jawahar Rojgar Yojna (JRY), an employment-generation programme for rural areas (named after the first prime minister of India, Jawaharlal

Nehru). With the help of the Development Support Centre, the KTGSM prepared a proposal for scientific development of watersheds. The project, covering 35 villages of Savarkundla *taluka,* had two components: It was proposed to build water harvesting structures on farmlands and adjoining public land to increase the rainfall retention for augmenting water supply for irrigation and drinking purposes and second, a land development programme was to be initiated in five identified micro watersheds.

The project was estimated to cost Rs 30 million over three years. In all, 12 percolation tanks, 14 check dams and 760 gully/*nalla* plugs or *bandharas* were to be constructed, an area of about 3,500 ha. was to be treated, and 300,000 trees were to be planted. An estimated 890,000 person-days of employment were to be generated to benefit more than 7,000 families.

The Objective

The objective of the project was to develop not only physical infrastructure but also management systems and village institutions through participatory processes for sustainable development and use of water resources to improve the income generating capacity and quality of life of the rural communities in the *taluka.*

Implementation

The project was sanctioned in September 1994. It was executed by a relatively small team of 15 members including the project co-ordinator and four engineers. The estimated total administrative cost was 7.5 per cent of the cost of works. The project activities were planned and executed between September 1994 and June 1998 because monsoon sets in around June end, after which no work is possible. Since most of the work was over by the first year itself, second year onwards the activities slowed down. Performance in terms of the construction of the physical structures was spectacular.

During the second year, planning for land shaping also

began. Initially, eight villages, where construction of water conservation structures was complete, were selected. The actual work of land shaping started in the third year and by June 1998, a total of 3,711 ha. were covered by contour bunding and trenches for drains; 121,800 saplings were planted to improve tree cover. Approximately, Rs 25 million were spent on all these works. Compared to any similar government programme, this achievement was indeed spectacular.

The water conservation structures were designed to impound more than 100 MCFt of water. More than 1,900 wells are to be recharged. A total of about 9,786 ha. of land will be brought under assured irrigation. After the first year, there was significant improvement in the area under cotton, which is the most paying crop in the region, followed by groundnut. There are significant inter-village and intra-village differences in the yield of cotton owing to various factors. However, assured irrigation has improved the yield by half, on an average. This increase in yield may be attributed to timely and adequate supply of water which was possible because of recharged wells. The output of other *kharif* cereal crops such as *jowar* and *bajra* was also stabilised with support irrigation. The KTGSM has tried to collect some information on area and output of crops in project villages, but there are some methodological problems and, hence, it is not possible to quantify the impact of the project with a fair degree of precision. Indirect evidence, however, suggests that the income of farmers rose in most of the villages. In Mitiyala, for instance, for the first time in the history of the village, a contribution of Rs 28,000 was collected for a socio-religious function, 'Tulsi Vivaha', in which even the Muslim households participated. It was a result of good income earned by farmers from irrigated cotton (farmers in Mitiyala have built a check dam, 4 percolation tanks and 95 *bandharas* to recharge their wells).

Participation Process

Information about the project was disseminated to all the 35 project villages by the project team including the project co-ordinator. The latter is a very senior member of the KTGSM's core team and enjoys high credibility among the villagers. The villagers were asked to identify sites on or near their fields where water courses could be bunded or dammed. Once the sites were identified, farmers had to notify the project office in Savarkundla. One of the engineers then visited the selected sites, inspected them, consulted the leader of potential beneficiaries and gave technical clearance. The engineer came back and prepared a plan and cost estimate for the proposed work. The farmer leader was then informed about the estimate and was asked to deposit five per cent of the cost towards a maintenance fund to be maintained by the project office. When the amount was deposited a work order was issued to the farmer. The farmer was then to execute the work under the technical supervision of the project engineer. Upon completion of the work, the engineer measured the quantum of work done and estimated the actual cost. Eighty per cent of the measured cost was reimbursed to the farmer or the group of farmers who constructed the check dam/*bandhara*/ percolation tank. This ensured people's contribution of 20 per cent towards the work.

Under the project procedure the KTGSM motivated and organised people for the work. During the first year, execution of work assumed priority. During the second year, village committees were formed in all the 35 villages. The DSC has provided continuous critical feedback on participation processes and a methodology to measure it. An important contribution of the DSC has been the introduction of Participatory Rural Appraisal (PRA), first to analyze the village situation, to identify sites for water conservation structures and finally to encourage involvement of the people in the activity. PRA encouraged many usually silent persons to speak up. In all the project villages, at least one PRA exercise was conducted. Interestingly, the village committee members showed keen interest in the concept, planning, and implementation of water conservation structures. The usual run-of-the-mill political leaders were generally relegated to the back seat. In a number of villages new leadership emerged. The village committee comprised eight-to-ten members drawn from all castes and classes. Their main function was to visit and approve the sites suggested by farmers. Most of the committees were active during the planning and construction stage. In each village, at least one committee member took active interest in the project and assumed the entire responsibility of contacting farmers, visiting sites, obtaining consent from the group of beneficiaries, and helping to collect the five per cent contribution. Some enthusiastic committee members also helped the beneficiary farmers in the construction process without any personal gain. Similarly, neighbouring farmers also helped by supplying water at the construction sites (without any charge for electricity or diesel oil used to pump it). In some instances, farmers also permitted submergence of a part of their farm to facilitate the construction of a structure, especially in the case of percolation tanks.

Individual farmers had to assume responsibility for land shaping activity on their own farms. The farmers had to contribute 50 per cent of the total cost of land shaping, the upper limit of which was Rs 4,000 per ha. A farmer received a maximum subsidy of Rs 2,000 per ha.for his work, and had to contribute the rest. The implementation procedure was the same as was followed for water conservation structures. The project engineers visited fields, provided guidance regarding the location of contour bunds, and prepared cost estimates. Farmers then built the contour bunds and the engineer measured the work done. In 13 villages where the water conservation structures were completed, an area of 3,711 ha.was brought under land shaping.

Is the Performance of NGOs Better than Government's?

It was argued earlier that the contribution of NGOs to the process of development has been through quality work and its impact on other processes. The KTGSM story confirms this thesis. Let us look at the evidence.

Quality of Work

Over a period of two-and-a-half years, a total of more than 850 water conservation structures were constructed by the people including 97 check dams and percolation tanks. Most of these structures have withstood at least one monsoon, and some have withstood two. None of the check dams and percolation tanks has been damaged. In case of *nalla* plugs or *bandharas,* only 56 out of the 826 built were damaged. Most of them were rebuilt by the farmers and interestingly the entire repairing expenditure was borne by them. Some initial inexperience was probably responsible for the damage. A retired chief engineer of the Government of Gujarat, engaged as a consultant by the DSC, visited a large number of sites and besides suggesting additional engineering inputs, he also recorded his appreciation of the quality of construction by the farmers. The fact that the structures were not built by contractors seems to explain the excellent quality of construction.

Cost-Effectiveness

The works executed by the KTGSM and the people of Savarkundla *taluka* were cost-effective partly because the administrative cost of the project was only 7.5 per cent of the total, as compared to the usual 20 per cent when handled by government departments. The compensation to staff in voluntary agencies is much lower than that given by the government. The KTGSM was no exception. The project co-ordinator accepted an honorarium of only Rs 3,000 per month, and that too, after the first year. Project engineers were paid between Rs 2,500 to Rs 4,500 per month, and the rest of the staff was paid Rs 1,200 to 2,000 per month. In a way the NGO sector provides subsidised service to society by accepting lower remuneration than offered in government departments (the latter is more than the opportunity cost if [eft to market forces). A pertinent question is whether the NGO sector should underpay its staff, all of whom may not share the voluntary spirit. Looking at the quality and quantity of work accomplished by the NGO sector, payment of market-based remuneration to its staff could become an added incentive for an expansion of its activities, if the requisite resources can be raised.

Second, no government department could have accomplished in two-and-a-half years as much as KTGSM. It took less than a week to prepare the plans and estimates for check dams and percolation tanks. In the case of *nalla* plugs, they were prepared within a day or two. Such speed is inconceivable in a departmental framework. It would have taken months to design and technically approve the same number of structures by a government department. Obviously, such speed raises cost-effectiveness. The KTGSM engineers did not have all the skills necessary for conducting technical surveys and preparing plans and estimates at the beginning and the DSC provided frequent guidance in the field as well as in the office. The project engineers were also trained in special training workshops. On the basis of its field experience, the DSC standardised certain designs and related calculations and put them on the computer to make them easily accessible to the KTGSM computers. The standardised formats were then installed in the KTGSM computers. This input from the DSC added significantly to speed and accuracy in designing, calculations, and billing. Further, the estimates were prepared on the basis of the 'Schedule of Rates (SOR)' approved by the government. The people contributed 20 per cent of the estimated cost of the structure in cash, kind, or through labour; but the total cost of most of the works was less than the initial estimates. In effect there was a saving of resources. Generally, in drought-prone areas, the contractors quote above the tender rates which are computed using the SOR, and the government approves such higher quotations. Had the government tried to implement the same project in Savarkundla by itself, several contracts would have been awarded at significantly higher rates.

Sustainability

As noted earlier the structures are technically sound. Since farmers have themselves built them to augment the water supply in their own wells, they undoubtedly take good care of them. In a few instances where the structures were damaged, the farmers and the members of the team reached the site and tried to repair the damages as soon as possible. In fact, the farmers have realised that there is hardly any effective alternative to the managing of natural resources than the one suggested to them by the KTGSM. Hence, the probability of sustaining the current method of resource conservation and management in the area is quite high. The land shaping work will help reduce soil erosion in the fields and the *bandharas,* check dams and percolation tanks will raise the water table.

Participation by the people has been fairly good. Women are yet to participate actively in decision-making processes; however, their participation by way of providing family labour and as hired labour for building the structures was substantial. A total of 400,429 person-days of employment was generated, of which women accounted for about 40 per cent. As stated earlier, the project has brought about a change in the leadership in many villages, and because the new leaders are attracted towards development, it is likely that the interest in project activities will survive in the long run.

Concluding Remarks

The KTGSM's case shows that a credible NGO with appropriate and adequate professional inputs and training (through the DSC in this case) can plan and execute a government programme that has been languishing for decades, and achieve a sustainable impact. Watershed development is not a new programme for the government. It has existed for a long time in one form or another, with various departments. However, the government programme has not been able to make much of an impact. In fact, obtaining consent for land shaping and creating small surface water conservation structures with the help of the village community has always proved difficult. The successful attempt by the KTGSM should create pressure on the government to encourage and support many similar experiemnts throughout the country.

REFERENCES

Arya, Ved (1996). *Towards a Relationship of Significance.* New Delhi: PRADAN.

Bhatt, Anil (1995). 'Voluntary action in India', *Economic and Political Weekly,* Vol. 30, No. 16, pp 870-76.

Fernandez, Aloysius P. (1996). *Working with Government.* Bangalore: MYRADA (Mysore Resettlement and Development Agency).

Ferrington, John and Anthony Babington (1993). *Reluctant Partners.* New York: Routledge.

Gulati, Ravi and Kaval Gulati (1996). *Strengthening Voluntary Action in India.* Delhi: Konark.

Pandey, S.R. (1991). *Community Action for Social Change: Grassroots Organisations in India.* New Delhi: Sage Publications.

CHAPTER 8

Role of Voluntary Organisations in Social Development

> When you have an accident, they will save their own people, and those who have worked with you or with the NGOs are left. Unfortunately, this happens always. It is not an excuse at all.
>
> —*Boutros Boutros-Ghali*

In India, the above categories of organisations and their evolutionary development are clearly seen in our recorded history right from the Buddhistic times or even earlier. They have been recorded in detail in Chanakya's *Arthashastra,* written around circa 325 B.C. India has a very long, ancient and traditional background of voluntary organisations and voluntary leadership, at times even based on elected leadership that sounds very ultra-modern. Before proceeding to discuss the contemporary international scene and the current national situation of voluntary organisations, let me discuss our own past and the institutions inherited by us, almost intact, from times immemorial, which have been either adopted or adapted to suit the needs and requirements of our modern democratic framework. In seriatum, of all the grassroots institutions at the village level, the first one was the Panchayat—"the Five First-Men" of the village.

Even the most ancient Tamil work (around the Christian era, "The Epic of the Anklet") *Silappadikaram* refers to it as "Iym-paeraayam" or the Five Member Committee. Strangely enough, in the Chola days, they were elected by secret ballot called, "Kudavolai", where the word "Kudam" refers to the ballot-box and the word "Olai" refers to the ballot-paper. Here, we find the non-governmental voluntary committee, introducing an electoral system of its own, replacing the erstwhile hereditary system. Apart from the Panchayat, the system of the village office, the village school (known as the Gurukul) system, the temple trust or the endowment and the village artisan-guild (Sreni) and the commercial guild, (Sreshti) all of them, in spite of the several changes of ruling power-groups, have remained more or less intact even to this day, albeit with some superficial cosmetic changes.

Terry Allibund in his book *Catalysts of Development—Voluntary Organisations in India, 1983,* reviews briefly India's recent historical record and its past development successes and failures in the field of PVOs, i.e. what be labels as "Private Voluntary Organisations", According to him, from an historical perspective, India's PVOs have provided a valuable series of unplanned (and largely unanalysed) socio-economic change-experiments. Hatch's work with the YMCA in rural Kerala, Elmhirst and Tagore's efforts with Bengali peasants, the early Christian missionary colonies in the North-west region, Bryane's authoritarian approach to change in Gurgaon District, Gandhiji's programme intended as a model for the rural development of independent India, and Mayer's demonstration of successful social and economic change at Etawah, are all cases that provide one of the richest sources of insight on appropriate and feasible development-methods in India.

Terry Allibund uses the words—"Voluntaryism" and "Volunteerism"—quite distinctly, the former meaning an institutional movement, and the latter pointing out individual initiative. Of the urges that propel people to voluntary action, Rajni Kothari observes: "The process of secularisation of power in place of the traditional ascriptive basis of power has generated two opposite forces: the few groups that were able to enter the political terrain and had the necessary means to retain their new-found position in the secular order have been possessed by a great sense of power and ascendancy, while the large majority of citizens whose aspirations have been aroused by the values of the democratic system but who did not have the necessary means to realise them have been possessed by a sense of inferiority, powerlessness and discontent. This is the great hiatus which divides the Indian people."

Dr. B.G. Verghese has drawn attention to a movement within the Catholic Church in Kerala that interprets true religion as a struggle for bread, human dignity, and social justice. He likens that movement to what he calls "the new awareness within the Gandhian movement", which focusses on "struggle" and on "organising the poor to overthrow the bonds of dead habit and vested interests of every kind". In another context, J. Duncan Derrett has shown the many ways in which a combination of constitutional provisions, public opinion and law, are forcing a number of previously idle Hindu religious endowments to be invested in educational and charitable endeavours that often end up promoting voluntary work with development objectives, such as in the case of the Ramakrishna Mission. Amongst such early endeavours, stand the most notable of such projects headed by Rabindranath Tagore in North Bengal, by Dr. Spencer Hatch at Marthandam in Madras, by F.L.Bryane in Gurgaon, Haryana, and by Sir V.T. Krishnamachari in the old princely state of Baroda. Both the Christian and the Hindu organisations, since Independence, have taken upon themselves the leadership-role in voluntary movements.

Swami Sivananda's Divine Life Society spearheaded social and medical programmes. So does the Satya Sai movement all over India. The proceeds of the Indira Gandhi Award for International Understanding were donated by Swami Ranganadananda for tribal welfare programmes in Bastar District of Madhya Pradesh. Government developmental programmes also increasingly came to be implemented by registered voluntary agencies of beneficiaries at the district level. Girijan Development Agency of Srikakulam District of Andhra Pradesh was the first of its kind in this regard for tribal development as a pace-setter as early as 1970.

Most modern Indian social theorists have attempted to find a way to preserve the warmth and intimate social relationships associated with traditional Indian social institutions while introducing greater degrees of equality within and between different groups. This effort is prominently reflected in the Indian Constitution, which as Galanter points out, "sets forth a general programme for the reconstruction of Indian society. It clearly sets out to secure to individuals equality of status and opportunity, to abolish invidious distinctions among groups, to protect the integrity and give free play to voluntary associations, (and to provide) the widest freedom of association to the individual and generally the widest personal freedom compatible with the public good." In general, the Government of India has taken, a cooperative stance toward voluntary associations, although it has been clear that foreign and international agencies are to operate within the country only under close supervision and monitoring. As observed by Marcus Franda in his *Voluntary Associations and Local Development in India: The Janata Phase,* "Continuity of this policy was confirmed dramatically in June 1978 when eight foreign members of the American-based Institute of Cultural Affairs were asked to leave the country after President Sanjiva Reddy had raised questions about why so many foreigners were participating in a rural development project in Maliwada, Maharashtra.

Caution about foreign agencies is in some measure a reflection of India's general nationalist distrust of the activities of outsiders in the country, but it is also a function of Indian leaders' intense conviction that the nation must nourish its own developmental and relief capabilities. This was clearly President Reddy's concern when he visited Maliwada in 1978." Voluntary organisations in India have also become professionalised because they have built up a corpus of specialised knowledge and experience about what does and does not work in bringing about socio-economic change. Such knowledge is only in small measure the preserve of technicians and scientists—geologists, well-drillers, agronomists, engineers, veterinarians, bankers, doctors and so forth—within these organisations.

Much of it lies within the domains of economics, sociology,

psychology, anthropology, communications, education, management, political science, law and other "softer" disciplines, all of which are also represented. Needless to say, graduates of professional schools and universities still prefer to go into government work, or into private or public sector industry; but the number who opt for participation in voluntary agencies is increasing. Realising the above hometruth, successive governments have laid great emphasis on voluntary organisations. From "Family Planning" to "Antyodaya", the conspectus is complete.

As Marcus Franda observes, "The fact that both Jawaharlal Nehru and Indira Gandhi have contributed to the, mushroom growth of local initiatives in the rural areas despite their emphasis on heavy industry and capital-intensive development-strategy for the nation as a whole brings home the point that almost everyone in India favours at least some degree of emphasis on Voluntary Organisations for rural growth." Today we have homes for adoption of children, shelter-homes for harassed wives, "Sumaitri Crisis" Centre at New Delhi for counselling, Senior Citizens' Resorts supported by Helpage, "Sisters of Charity" running a chain of institutions all over India, attracting the young and the old alike. In the field of welfare and rural development, there are many who look down upon the so-called "Subsidy-culture". Here one must remember that the Green Revolution would not have been a great success but for the largescale subsidisation of inputs even for the big farmer — particularly the chemical and mechanical inputs — as well as concessional interest on borrowings.

Subsidisation of Voluntary Organisations particularly in the field of Weaker Sections' Welfare is very important, provided it is ensured that assistance reaches the target-groups. For this, mass-opinionisation through motivation and campaign is required, and this can be achieved only through Voluntary Organisations. Nevertheless, self-reliance on simple needs and requirements can, be brought about at the local level only through cottage-door education. Here again, self reliance plays a role. Regarding "Village-Self-Reliance" Shri

Kailash Nath Katju, the then Chief Minister of Madhya Pradesh, observed in 1953:

> I am convinced that the problem is not so much of money as of men. In our villages we have enormous manpower...Let every villager clean his house and his lanes once every month.... The villagers should also beautify their villages and homes. There are hundreds of simple ways in which real beauty can be achieved. It is by no means a costly affair.... Their salvation lies in their own hands, and unless they gird up their loins to help themselves, Government will not be able to infuse life and energy into rural development work... The only thing that is required is discipline and organisation and a spirit of service on the part of the leading villagers in each village.

Self-reliance is the sheet-anchor of Voluntaryism. It is sad but true that the so called "leading villagers" invest their surpluses in cities and *not* at their homes and hamlets, mainly because real estate appreciates much faster in urban centres. Government investment alone cannot clean up and beautify our villages, as our priorities right now, are drinking water, immunisation and nutrition, which can also be promoted by Voluntary Organisations.

In India there have been different systems of assistance to voluntary organisations. The assistance may be advanced by the Central or State Governments concerned either directly or through their undertakings, corporations or autonomous bodies. This may be advanced either to totally private voluntary organisations or such other registered societies that are headed by certain district authorities. With regard to funding from abroad, this may directly go to the voluntary organisations concerned, i.e. those registered with the Home Ministry for receiving such funds under the Reserve Bank surveillance. We have been having a number of programmes of assistance to voluntary organisations right from the mid-fifties such as Freedom-form Hunger Campaign (FFHC), Action for Food

Programme (ACFO), People's Action for Development (PADE), and quite recently the Centre for Appropriate Technology (CART). Now, there is only one central and controlling agency of channeling the foreign financial assistance to voluntary organisations all over India, namely the CAPART which has merged both the "Appropriate Technology" and "People's Action". The CAPART thus becomes the sole arbiter of selection of the voluntary organisations. For example, the Indian Red Cross which is a statutory body is considered a voluntary organisation whereas the National Institute of Social Action which comprises 22 non-officials out of the entire 33 -member committee is not considered a voluntary organisation by the CAPART, although both the Red Cross and the NISA have the concerned Governor as the Ex-officio-President. This study itself is a result of the Convention organised by the NISA. The list of participants, both individual and institutional, would clearly show the totally voluntary and non-governmental nature of the organisation which the CAPART has not considered as "Voluntary".

The self-same CAPART considers registered societies headed by the District Collectors as voluntary organisations! I am sure, such anomalies could be eliminated if there is proper screening and better understanding of the voluntary nature of the organisations concerned. This book is a step in this direction, bringing together on the same forum hundreds of smaller voluntary organisations under the banner of an apex body called "NISA". The most outstanding contribution of any statutory body on voluntary organisations is forthcoming from the report of the Kudal Commission, which said that to give a fillip to the voluntary movement in the country as also for providing work, necessary legislative provisions needed to be introduced to prevent individuals from holding key positions in more than a specified number of voluntary organisations at a time. The Commission called for periodic physical verification of projects undertaken by them with Governmental assistance.

Besides, introduction of "deterrent punishment" for misuse and misappropriation of funds meant for the poor, the destitute and the needy sections of society, would also help in arresting the present trend. It is said that there was a need to review all the schemes under which funds are released to voluntary organisations by the Government departments and autonomous bodies. It also asked the Government departments not to release the funds at the eleventh hour as the benefits did not reach the poor.

The Kudal Commission urged the Government to make suitable legislative provisions either to stop the entry of foreign funds in the country through voluntary organisations or to regulate their inflow through Government channels only, and keep a close watch over their utilisation. The Commission said that the Government ought to preclude voluntary agencies getting involved in any clandestine and anti-national activities especially in the restricted areas of the country, and that the Government should review its policy pertaining to mapping and surveying of such areas, especially the aerial photography by private individuals or organisations and make relevant statutory provisions to put an end to this practice.

The role of voluntary organisations in the international field has been greatly enlarged during this century. Apart from the International Red Cross in the field of relief and rehabilitation, and the United Nations and its allied international bodies in the field of peacekeeping and development, we have been witnessing a tremendous spurt of international voluntary bodies like the Rotary, the Lions, the Jaycees and so on, not to speak of the time-honoured Free Masons' Lodge. In the field of religion and philosophy, education and philanthropy, trade and commerce, professionalism and journalism, sports and games; there have been an unanimous universal response to voluntary effort and, voluntary participation. The Olympics and the Asiad are examples of this exemplary progress towards voluntary unification of nations and towards a world brotherhood. If only we enumerate names of all organisations under each category mentioned here and their work in their respective fields, it will literally and metaphorically speak volumes of voluntary human organisations spanning a wide variety of human endeavour towards individual and collective human happiness. This is what Milton had on his mind's eye—an almost Kaleidoscopic procession of harmonious voluntary actions ranging from the ecology of the flora and the fauna, to dignity of humanism and the divinity of man.

REFERENCES

Hill, Michael, 1980, *Understanding Social Policy,* Oxford: Basil Blackwell.

Kahn, Robert L., 1964, *Organisational Stress: Studies in Role Conflict and Ambiguity,* New York: John Wiley.

Kasona. George, 1960, *The Powerful Consumer: Psychological Studies of the American Economy,* New York: McGraw-Hill.

Rubington, Earl, and Martin S. Weinberg, eds., 1977, *The Study of Social Problems: Five Perspectives,* New York: Oxford University Press.

Shaw, Clifford, Henry Mckay, et al., 1929, *Delinquency Areas: A Study of the Geographical Distribution of School Truants, Juvenile Delinquents and Adult Offenders in Chicago,* Chicago: University of Chicago press.

CHAPTER 9

Role of Voluntary Sector in India

> A multitude of causes unknown to former times are now acting with a combined force to blunt the discriminating powers of the mind, and unfitting it for all voluntary exertion to reduce it to a state of almost savage torpor.
>
> —*William Wordsworth*

Non-governmental organisation (NGO) is a term that has become widely accepted as referring to a legally constituted, non-governmental organisation created by natural or legal persons with no participation or representation of any government. In the cases in which NGOs are funded totally or partially by governments, the NGO maintains its non-governmental status and excludes government representatives from membership in the organisation. Unlike the term *intergovernmental organisation*, "non-governmental organisation" is a term in general use but is not a legal definition. In many jurisdictions these types of organisation are defined as "civil society organisations" or referred to by other names. The number of internationally operating NGOs is estimated at 40,000. National numbers are even higher: Russia has 277,000 NGOs. India is estimated to have between 1 million and 2 million NGOs.

National NGOs go back to antiquity. International non-governmental organisations have a history dating back to at least 1839. Rotary, later Rotary International, was founded in 1905. It has been estimated that by 1914 there were 1083

NGOs. International NGOs were important in the anti-slavery movement and the movement for women's suffrage, and reached a peak at the time of the World Disarmament Conference. However, the phrase "non-governmental organisation" only came into popular use with the establishment of the United Nations Organisation in 1945 with provisions in Article 71 of Chapter 10 of the United Nations Charter for a consultative role for organisations which are neither governments nor member states—see Consultative Status.

The definition of "international NGO" (INGO) is first given in resolution 288 (X) of ECOSOC on February 27, 1950: it is defined as "any international organisation that is not founded by an international treaty". The vital role of NGOs and other "major groups" in sustainable development was recognised in Chapter 27 of Agenda 21, leading to intense arrangements for a consultative relationship between the United Nations and non-governmental organisations. Rapid development of the non-governmental sector occurred in western countries as a result of the processes of restructurisation of the welfare state. Further globalisation of that process occurred after the fall of the communist system and was an important part of the Washington consensus.

Globalisation during the 20th century gave rise to the importance of NGOs. Many problems could not be solved within a nation. International treaties and international organisations such as the World Trade Organisation were perceived as being too centred on the interests of capitalist enterprises. Some argued that in an attempt to counterbalance this trend, NGOs have developed to emphasize humanitarian issues, developmental aid and sustainable development. A prominent example of this is the World Social Forum which is a rival convention to the World Economic Forum held annually in January in Davos, Switzerland. The fifth World Social Forum in Porto Alegre, Brazil, in January 2005 was attended by representatives from more than 1,000 NGOs. Some have argued that in forums like these, NGOs take the place of what should belong to popular movements of the poor. Others argue that NGOs are often imperialist in nature, that they sometimes operate in a racialised manner in dominant countries, and that they fulfil a similar function to that of the clergy during the high colonial era. The philosopher Peter Hallward argues that they are an aristocratic form of politics. However, this philosophy would suggest that organisations of indigenous peoples are not represented, which is untrue. Whatever the case, NGO transnational networking is now extensive.

Types of NGOs

Apart from "NGO", often alternative terms are used as for example: independent sector, volunteer sector, civil society, grassroots organisations, transnational social movement organisations, private voluntary organisations, self-help organisations and non-state actors (NSA's). Non-governmental organisations are a heterogeneous group. A long list of acronyms has developed around the term "NGO".

These include:

- CSO, short for civil society organisation;
- DONGO: Donor Organised NGO;
- ENGO: short for environmental NGO, such as Global 2000;
- GONGOs are government-operated NGOs, which may have been set up by governments to look like NGOs in order to qualify for outside aid or promote the interests of the government in question;
- INGO stands for international NGO; Oxfam is an international NGO
- QUANGOs are quasi-autonomous non-governmental organisations, such as the International Organisation for Standardisation (ISO). (The ISO is actually not purely an NGO, since its membership is by nation, and each nation is represented by what the ISO Council determines to be the 'most broadly representative' standardisation body of a nation. That body might itself be a nongovernmental organisation;

for example, the United States is represented in ISO by the American National Standards Institute, which is independent of the federal government. However, other countries can be represented by national governmental agencies; this is the trend in Europe.)

- TANGO: short for technical assistance NGO;
- GSO: Grassroots Support Organisation
- MANGO: short for market advocacy NGO.

There are also numerous classifications of NGOs. The typology the World Bank uses divides them into Operational and Advocacy:

> *The primary purpose of an operational NGO is the design and implementation of development-related projects. One frequently used categorisation is the division into relief-oriented versus development-oriented organisations; they can also be classified according to whether they stress service delivery or participation; or whether they are religious or secular; and whether they are more public or private-oriented. Operational NGOs can be community-based, national or international.*

The primary purpose of an Advocacy NGO is to defend or promote a specific cause. As opposed to operational project management, these organisations typically try to raise awareness, acceptance and knowledge by lobbying, press work and activist events. USAID refers to NGOs as *private voluntary organisations*. However many scholars have argued that this definition is highly problematic as many NGOs are in fact state and corporate funded and managed projects with professional staff. Furthermore it has often been argued that USAID is in fact a key arm of American imperialism and that it sets up and supports NGOs in order to further imperial agendas. NGOs exist for a variety of reasons, usually to further the political or social goals of their members or funders. Examples include improving the state of the natural environment, encouraging the observance of human rights, improving the welfare of the disadvantaged, or representing a corporate agenda. However, there are a huge number of such organisations and their goals cover a broad range of political and philosophical positions. This can also easily be applied to private schools and athletic organisations.

Methods

NGOs vary in their methods. Some act primarily as lobbyists, while others primarily conduct programmes and activities. For instance, an NGO such as Oxfam, concerned with poverty alleviation, might provide needy people with the equipment and skills to find food and clean drinking water, whereas an NGO like the FFDA helps through investigation and documentation of human rights violations and provides legal assistance to victims of human rights abuses. Others, such as Afghanistan Information Management Services, provide specialised technical products and services to support development activities implemented on the ground by other organisations.

Public Relations

Non-governmental organisations need healthy relationships with the public to meet their goals. Foundations and charities use sophisticated public relations campaigns to raise funds and employ standard lobbying techniques with governments. Interest groups may be of political importance because of their ability to influence social and political outcomes.

Consulting

Project management: There is an increasing awareness that management techniques are crucial to project success in non-governmental organisations. Generally, non-governmental organisations that are private have either a community or environmental focus. They address varieties of issues such as religion, emergency aid, or humanitarian affairs. They mobilize public support and voluntary contributions for aid; they often have strong links with community groups in developing countries, and they often work in areas where government-to-government aid is not possible. NGOs are accepted as a part of the international relations landscape, and while they influence national and multilateral policy-making, increasingly they are more directly involved in local action.

Staffing

Not all people working for non-governmental organisations are volunteers. The reasons people volunteer are not necessarily purely altruistic, and can provide immediate benefits for themselves as well as those they serve, including skills, experience, and contacts. There is some dispute as to whether expatriates should be sent to developing countries. Frequently this type of personnel is employed to satisfy a donor who wants to see the supported project managed by someone from an industrialised country. However, the expertise these employees or volunteers may have can be counterbalanced by a number of factors: the cost of foreigners is typically higher, they have no grassroot connections in the country they are sent to, and local expertise is often undervalued. The NGO sector is an important employer in terms of numbers. For example, by the end of 1995, CONCERN worldwide, an international Northern NGO working against poverty, employed 174 expatriates and just over 5,000 national staff working in ten developing countries in Africa and Asia, and in Haiti.

Funding

Large NGOs may have annual budgets in the hundreds of millions or billions of dollars. For instance, the budget of the American Association of Retired Persons (AARP) was over US$540 million in 1999. Funding such large budgets demands significant fundraising efforts on the part of most NGOs. Major sources of NGO funding include membership dues, the sale of goods and services, grants from international institutions or national governments, and private donations. Several EU-grants provide funds accessible to NGOs. Even though the term "non-governmental organisation" implies independence from governments, most NGOs depend heavily on governments for their funding. A quarter of the US$162 million income in

1998 of the famine-relief organisation Oxfam was donated by the British government and the EU. The Christian relief and development organisation World Vision collected US$55 million worth of goods in 1998 from the American government. Nobel Prize winner Médecins Sans Frontières (MSF) (known in the USA as Doctors Without Borders) gets 46% of its income from government sources.

Monitoring and Control

In a March 2000 report on United Nations Reform priorities, former U.N. Secretary General Kofi Annan wrote in favour of international humanitarian intervention, arguing that the international community has a "right to protect" citizens of the world against ethnic cleansing, genocide, and crimes against humanity. On the heels of the report, the Canadian government launched the Responsibility to Protect R2PPDF (434 KiB) project, outlining the issue of humanitarian intervention. While the R2P doctrine has wide applications, among the more controversial has been the Canadian government's use of R2P to justify its intervention and support of the coup in Haiti. Years after R2P, the World Federalist Movement, an organisation which supports "the creation of democratic global structures accountable to the citizens of the world and call for the division of international authority among separate agencies", has launched Responsibility to Protect-Engaging Civil Society (R2PCS). A collaboration between the WFM and the Canadian government, this project aims to bring NGOs into lockstep with the principles outlined under the original R2P project.

The governments of the countries an NGO works or is registered in may require reporting or other monitoring and oversight. Funders generally require reporting and assessment, such information is not necessarily publicly available. There may also be associations and watchdog organisations that research and publish details on the actions of NGOs working in particular geographic or programme areas. In recent years, many large corporations have increased their corporate social responsibility departments in an attempt to preempt NGO campaigns against certain corporate practices. As the logic goes, if corporations work *with* NGOs, NGOs will not work *against* corporations. In December 2007, The United States Department of Defence Assistant Secretary of Defence (Health Affairs) established an International Health Division under Force Health Protection & Readiness.

Part of International Health's mission is to communicate with NGOs in areas of mutual interest. Department of Defence Directive 3000.05, in 2005, requires DoD to regard stability-enhancing activities as a mission of importance equal to warfighting. In compliance with international law, DoD has necessarily built a capacity to improve essential services in areas of conflict such as Iraq, where the customary lead agencies (State Department and USAID) find it difficult to operate. Unlike the "co-option" strategy described for corporations, the OASD(HA) recognises the neutrality of health as an essential service. International Health cultivates collaborative relationships with NGOs, albeit at arms-length, recognising their traditional independence, expertise and honest broker status. While the goals of DoD and NGOs may seem incongruent, the DoD's emphasis on stability and security to reduce and prevent conflict suggests, on careful analysis, important mutual interests.

Legal Status

The legal form of NGOs is diverse and depends upon homegrown variations in each country's laws and practices. However, four main family groups of NGOs can be found worldwide:

- Unincorporated and voluntary association
- Trusts, charities and foundations
- Companies not just for profit
- Entities formed or registered under special NGO or nonprofit laws.

NGOs are not subjects of international law, as states are. An exception is the International Committee of the Red Cross, which is subject to certain specific matters, mainly relating to the Geneva Convention. The Council of Europe in Strasbourg drafted the European Convention on the Recognition of the Legal Personality of International Non-Governmental Organisations in 1986, which sets a common legal basis for the existence and work of NGOs in Europe. Article 11 of the European Convention on Human Rights protects the right to freedom of association, which is also a fundamental norm for NGOs.

Citizen Organisation

There is a growing movement within the "non"-profit and "non"-government sector to define itself in a more constructive, accurate way. Instead of being defined by "non" words, organisations are suggesting new terminology to describe the sector. The term "civil society organisation" (CSO) has been used by a growing number of organisations, such as the Centre for the Study of Global Governance. The term "citizen sector organisation" (CSO) has also been advocated to describe the sector — as one of citizens, for citizens. This labels and positions the sector as its own entity, without relying on language used for the government or business sectors. However some have argued that this is not particularly helpful given that most NGOs are in fact funded by governments and business and that some NGOs are clearly hostile to independently organised people's organisations.

Non-profit Organisation

A nonprofit organisation (abbreviated NPO, also not-for-profit) is an organisation that does not distribute its surplus funds to owners or shareholders, but instead uses them to help pursue its goals. Examples of NPOs include charities (i.e. charitable organisations), trade unions, and public arts organisations. Most governments and government agencies meet this definition, but in most countries they are considered a separate type of organisation and not counted as NPOs.

Non-profit Distinction

Whereas for-profit organisations exist to earn and re-distribute taxable wealth to employees and shareholders, the nonprofit corporation exists solely to provide programmes and services that are of self-benefit. Often these programmes, services and policies are overlooked and not otherwise executed or enforced by the government. While they are able to earn a surplus, more accurately called a profit, such earnings must be retained by the organisation for its self-preservation, expansion and future plans. Earnings may not benefit individuals or stake-holders. While some nonprofit organisations put substantial funds into hiring and rewarding their internal corporate leadership, middle-management personnel and workers, others employ unpaid volunteers and even executives may work for no compensation.

However, since the late 1980s there has been a growing consensus that nonprofits can achieve their corporate targets more effectively by using some of the same methods developed in for-profit enterprises. These include effective internal management, ensuring accountability for results, and monitoring the performance of different divisions or projects in order to better benefit from their capital and workers. Those require satisfied management and that, in turn, begins with the organisation's mission.

Nature and Goals

NPOs are often charities or service organisations; they may be organised as a not-for-profit corporation or as a trust, a cooperative, or they may be purely informal. Sometimes they are also called foundations, or endowments that have large stock funds. A very similar organisation called the supporting organisation operates like a foundation, but they are more complicated to administer, they are more tax favoured, and the public charities that receive grants from them must have a specially determined relationship. Foundations give out grants to other NPOs, or fellowships and direct grants to participants. However, the name *foundations* may be used by any not-for-profit corporation — even volunteer organisations or grass roots groups. Applying Germanic or Nordic law (e.g., Germany, Sweden, Finland), NPOs typically are voluntary associations, although some have a corporate structure (e.g. housing cooperatives). Usually a voluntary association is founded upon the principle of one-person-one-vote.

Legal Aspects

There is a wide diversity of structures and purposes in the NPO landscape. For legal classification and eventual scrutiny, there are, nevertheless, some structural elements of prime legal importance:

- Economic activity
- Supervision and management provisions
- Representation
- Accountability and Auditing provisions
- Provisions for the amendment of the statutes or articles of incorporation
- Provisions for the dissolution of the entity
- Tax status of corporate and private donors
- Tax status of the foundation.

Some of the above must be, in most jurisdictions, expressed in the document of establishment. Others may be provided by the supervising authority at each particular jurisdiction. While affiliations will not affect a legal status, they may be taken into consideration in legal proceedings as an indication of purpose. Most countries have laws which regulate the establishment and management of NPOs, and which require compliance with corporate governance regimes. Most larger organisations are required to publish their financial reports detailing their income and expenditure for the public. In many aspects they are similar to business entities though there are often significant differences. Both non-profit and for-profit entities must have board members, steering committee members, or trustees who owe the organisation a fiduciary duty of loyalty and trust. A notable exception to this involves churches, which are often not required to disclose finances to anyone, including church members, though most churches remain fiscally transparent with their members.

Formation and Structure

In the United States, nonprofit organisations are formed by incorporating in the state in which they expect to do business. The act of incorporating creates a legal entity enabling the organisation to be treated as a corporation under law and to enter into business dealings, form contracts, and own property as any other individual or for-profit corporation may do. Nonprofits can have members but many do not. The nonprofit may also be a trust or association of members. The organisation may be controlled by its members who elect the Board of Directors, Board of Governors or Board of Trustees. Nonprofits may have a delegate structure to allow for the representation of groups or corporations as members. Alternately, it may be a non-membership organisation and the board of directors may elect its own successors. A primary difference between a nonprofit and a for-profit corporation is that a nonprofit does not issue stock or pay dividends, (for example, The Code of the Commonwealth of Virginia includes the Non-Stock Corporation Act that is used to incorporate nonprofit entities) and may not enrich its directors. However, like for-profit corporations, nonprofits may still have employees and can compensate their directors within reasonable bounds.

The two major types of nonprofit organisation structure are membership and board-only. A membership organisation elects the board and has regular meetings and power to amend the bylaws. A board-only organisation typically has a self-selected board, and a membership whose powers are limited to those delegated to it by the board. A board-only organisation's bylaws may even state the organisation has no membership, although the organisation's literature may refer to its donors as "members"; examples of such structures are Fairvote and the National Organisation for the Reform of Marijuana Laws. The Model Nonprofit Corporation Act imposes many complexities and requirements on membership decision-making. Accordingly, many organisations, such as Wikimedia, have formed board-only structures. The National Association of Parliamentarians has raised concerns about the implications of this trend for the future of openness, accountability, and understanding of grassroots concerns in nonprofit organisations.

Specifically, they note that nonprofit organisations, unlike business corporations, are not subject to market discipline for products and shareholder discipline over their capital; therefore, without membership control of major decisions such as election of the board, there are few inherent safeguards against abuse. A rebuttal to this might be that as nonprofit organisations grow and seek larger donations, the level of scrutiny rises, including expectations of audited financial statements.

Tax Exemption

In many countries, nonprofits may apply for tax exempt status, so that the organisation itself may be exempt from income tax and other taxes. In the United States, to be exempt from federal income taxes the organisation must meet the requirements set forth by the Internal Revenue Service.

United States

After a recognised type of legal entity has been formed at the state level, it is customary for the nonprofit organisation to seek tax exempt status with respect to its income tax obligations. That is typically done by applying to the Internal Revenue Service (IRS), although statutory exemptions exist for limited types of nonprofit organisations. The IRS, after reviewing the application to ensure the organisation meets the conditions to be recognised as a tax exempt organisation (such as the purpose, limitations on spending, and internal safeguards for a charity), may issue an authorisation letter to the nonprofit granting it tax exempt status for income tax payment, filing, and deductibility purposes. The exemption does not apply to other Federal taxes such as employment taxes. Additionally, a tax-exempt organisation must pay federal tax on income that is unrelated to their exempt purpose. Failure to maintain operations in conformity to the laws may result in an organisation losing its tax exempt status. Individual states and localities offer nonprofits exemptions from other taxes such as sales tax or property tax. Federal tax-exempt status does not guarantee exemption from state and local taxes, and vice versa. These exemptions generally have separate application processes and their requirements may differ from the IRS requirements. Furthermore, even a tax exempt organisation may be required to file annual financial reports (IRS Form 990) at the state and federal level.

Finland

In Finland, "rekisteröity yhdistys", given the abbreviation ry, denotes a registered association. This is done at a cost of 50 Euro. The association is required by law to keep a list of members. It must also hold an AGM and at least 3 members are required to set it up. A secretary, chair and treasurer being the usual formation.

India

In India, NPOs are commonly known as Non-Governmental Organisations (NGOs). They can be registered in four ways, viz. 1. Trust 2. Society 3. Section-25 Company 4. Special Licensing. Registration can be done with the Registrar of Companies(RoC). The following laws or Constitutional Articles of the Republic of India are relevant to the NGOs:

- Articles 19(1)(c) and 30 of the Constitution of India
- Income Tax Act, 1961
- Public Trusts Acts of various states
- Societies Registration Act, 1860
- Section 25 of the Indian Companies Act, 1956
- Foreign Contribution (Regulation) Act, 1976.

Canada

In Canada, NPOs may be formed at either the federal or

provincial levels. Charities must generally be registered with the Canada Revenue Agency and may issue tax receipts for donations.

South Africa

In South Africa, charities issue a tax certificate when requested by donors which can be used as a tax deduction by the donor.

United Kingdom

In the UK, many non-profit companies are incorporated as a company limited by guarantee. This means that the company does not have shares or shareholders, but it has the benefits of corporate status. This includes limited liability for its members and being able to enter into contracts and purchase property in its own name. The goals ("objects") of the company are defined in the Memorandum of Association when the company is formed. The profits of the company (also referred to as the trading surplus) must be invested in achieving these goals and not distributed to the company's members. Alternatively, non-profit companies may be formed as a Community Interest Company. This is in many ways similar to a Limited Liability Company, but is intended specifically to ensure that the profits and assets of the company are used for public good. A charity is a non-profit organisation that meets stricter criteria regarding its purpose and the way in which it makes decisions and reports its finances.. For example, a charity is generally not allowed to pay its Trustees. In England and Wales, charities may be registered with the Charity Commission. In Scotland, the Office of the Scottish Charity Regulator serves the same function. Other organisations which are classified as non-profit organisations elsewhere, such as trade unions, are subject to separate regulations, and are not regarded as "charities" in the technical sense.

Issues Faced by NPOs

Capacity building is an ongoing problem faced by NPOs for a number of reasons. Most rely on external funding (government funds, grants from charitable foundations, direct donations) to maintain their operations and changes in these sources of revenue may influence the reliability or predictability with which the organisation can hire and retain staff, sustain facilities, or create programmes. In addition, unreliable funding, long hours and low pay can lead to employee burnout and high rates of turnover. Founder's syndrome is an issue organisations face as they grow. Dynamic founders with a strong vision of how to operate the project try to retain control over the organisation, even as new employees or volunteers want to expand the project's scope and try new things.

Examples

In the United States, two of the wealthiest non-profit organisations are the Bill and Melinda Gates Foundation, which has an endowment of $38 billion, and the Howard Hughes Medical Institute, which has an endowment of approximately $14.8 billion. Outside the United States, another large NPO is the British Wellcome Trust, which is a "charity" in British usage. Measuring an NPO by its monetary size has obvious limitations, as the power and significance of NPOs are defined by more qualitative measurements such as effectiveness at carrying out charitable mission and goals. Some NPOs which are particularly well known, often for the charitable or social nature of their activities conducted over a long period of time, include Amnesty International, the Better Business Bureau, Oxfam, Carnegie Corporation of New York, DEMIRA Deutsche Minenräumer (German Mine Clearers), Goodwill Industries, United Way, The National Rifle Association, ACORN, Habitat for Humanity, Teach For America, the Red Cross and Red Crescent organisations, UNESCO, IEEE, World Wide Fund for Nature, Heifer International, and SOS Children's Villages. However, there are also millions of smaller NPOs that provide social services and relief efforts on a more focused level (such as Crosswind — Community Outreach Ministry and Literacy Centre West) to people throughout the world. There are more than 1.6 million NPOs in the United States alone.

On the Internet

Many NPOs often use the.org or.us (or the CCTLD of their respective country) or.edu top-level domain (TLD) when selecting a domain name to differentiate themselves from more commercially focused entities which typically use the.com space. In the traditional domain categories as noted in RFC 1591,.org is for "organisations that didn't fit anywhere else" in the naming system, which implies that it is the proper category for non-commercial organisations if they are not governmental, educational, or one of the other types with a specific TLD. It is not specifically designated for charitable organisations or any specific organisational or tax-law status, however; it encompasses anything that does not fall into another category. Currently, no restrictions are enforced on registration of.com or.org, so you can find organisations of all sorts in either of these domains, as well as other top-level domains including newer, more-specific ones which may fit particular sorts of organisations such as.museum for museums or.coop for cooperatives. Organisations might also register under the appropriate country code top-level domain for their country.

Role of Non-governmental Organisations

Non-Governmental Organisations (NGOs) are becoming increasingly important in the field of development. NGOs are a very important link between people at the grassroots, civil society and the state. They are diverse both in terms of organisational form, structure and culture and in terms of the issues they cover. Their involvement is not only seen in the implementation of governmental programmes but also in the process of formulation of public policies, and even in the enforcement of social legislation. This unit will discuss Non-Governmental Organisations, their objectives, community support, projects and innovations and monitoring and evaluation with a view to understand their roles and responsibilities in the present context. According to Gangrade (2001) voluntary sector has always played an important role in society from time immemorial. The concept and approach in voluntary work has undergone many changes from time to time. From pure charity, relief and welfare oriented approach this sector has in recent times suitably modelled and equipped itself to meet the development needs of society. There is hardly any field which is not now touched by NGO sector/voluntary sector. The NGOs have acquired an important position in various fields at the national and international levels. In 1994., at the Cairo International Conference on Population and Development, Governments unanimously endorsed, through the programme of action, the need to promote an effective partnership between all levels of Government and the full range of non-governmental organisations, and local community groups in the discussion and decisions on the design, implementation, coordination, monitoring and evaluation of programmes relating to population, development and environment. In the Cairo Conference a call was made to the governments and donors to ensure that NGOs are able to maintain their capacities. In our country, the role of NGOs in various fields such as education, health, culture and social welfare has been increasingly recognised.

Hasheni (1990) is of the opinion that NGOs and their members are organised in such a manner that they appear to be participatory. There is a need to institutionalise the role of NGOs in various fields through strong policy directives and implementation of such directives must be ensured by the Government of India and State Governments. The voluntary sector earlier was confined to the role of the capacity building, awareness raising and mobilisation of the community. During present time NGOs are no longer confined to their traditional domain of health, education and welfare. Today they are also taking up sophisticated technical assignments in various technical fields like water resources, watershed, forestry, environment, Human Immuno-Virus (HIV) or Acquired Immune Deficiency Syndrome (AIDS), drug abuse and consumer rights. Alarge number of Indian NGOs is now manned by professionals and technocrats of high caliber. Under the changing scenario competent NGOs need to be involved in all the developmental fields, including technical fields. In the age of globalisation and consumerism when every field is being opened up for the industries, private sector and multi-nations, NGOs are also playing their important role especially in the field of social sector-education and health. The NGO sector has contributed significantly in finding innovative solutions to poverty, deprivation, social discrimination and social mobilisation. It also includes service delivery, training, research and advocacy. The NGO sector has been serving as an important non-political link between the people and the Government.

Concept and History

Commission of Non-Governmental Organisations (2000) defines a Non-Governmental Organisation (NGO) as any non profit, voluntary citizens' group which is organised at a local, national or international level. Task oriented and driven by people with a common interest, NGOs perform a variety of service and humanitarian functions, bring citizens' concerns to Government, advocate and monitor policies and encourage political participation through provision of information. Some are organised around specific issues, such as human rights, environment or health. Deborah (1997) specifies the role of NGOs in terms of the capacity building. The NGO sector has often been described as extremely diverse, heterogeneous and populated by organisations with hugely varied goals, structures and motivations. It is not easy to define an NGO. It cannot be based on any legal definition, given the wide variations in laws related to NGO activities. World Bank Operational Manual (1989) defines NGOs as organisations that are entirely or largely independent of government and characterised primarily by rather than commercial.

The terminology varies; for example, in the United States they are called, private voluntary organisations, and most African NGOs prefer the label, "Voluntary Development Organisations". These can beproduction related NGOs, consumer and credit cooperatives, charitable and religious associations. NGOs vary in terms of manpower and professional staff depending upon the number of objectives they carry out. Operational NGOs contribute to the delivery of services (such as in the field of welfare), whereas in the primary aim of advocacy an

NGO influences the policies of public authorities and public opinion in general Some of the characteristics shared by different NGOs are as follows:

- NGOs are independent, in particular, of government and other public authorities and of political parties or commercial organisations.
- They are accountable to their members, donors and even with the funding agencies in terms of programme planning and implementation.
- They have their own governing bodies, office bearers and the procedure for the election as per the Registrar of the Societies.
- NGOs are formed voluntarily and there is usually an element of voluntary participation in the organisation.
- NGOs are not created to generate personal profit. However, they receive grants, donations from national and international sources.
- NGOs are also called as 'voluntary organisations' or 'civil society organisations'.

A Non-Governmental Organisation is a legally constituted organisation created by private persons or organisations with no participation or representation of any government. In cases in which NGOs are funded totally or partially by governments, the NGO maintains its non-government status insofar as it excludes representatives from membership in the organisation. Globalisation during the 20th century gave rise to the importance of NGOs. lVGOs have evolved to emphasize humanitarian issues, developmental aid and sustainable development. Aprorninent example of this is the 'World Social Forum' which is a rival convention of World Economic Forum. The fifth World Social Forum in 2005 held in Brazil was attended by more 1000 NGOs including Indian NGOs. Registered Societies: Societies Registration Act 1860 is a Central Act for registering non-profit organisations. Almost all the states in India have adopted the Central Act for creating state level authorities for registering various types of non profit entities. According to the Act, any seven persons who subscribe to the

Memorandum of Association can register a society. The memorandum should include aims of society, its objectives, its names, addresses and occupation of the members. NGOs have a long history at the international level, dating back to mid 19" century. They were important in the anti-slavery movement and the movement of women's suffrage and reached a peak at the time of the world Disarmament Conference.

However, the phrase non-governmental organisation only came into Role of Non-Governmental popular use with the establishment of the United Nations organisation in 1945 Organisations with provisions in Article 71 of the chapter 10 of the United Nations charter, for a consultative role for organisations which are neither governmental nor the member states. The definition of International NGO is first given in resolution 288(x) in 1950 as any International organisation that is not founded by an International treaty. The vital role of NGOs was recognised in chapter 27 of Agenda 21. An NGO can be created for public charitable purposes. There is no all India Act for setting up public Charitable Trusts.

Some of the states in India have enacted the public Charitable Trust Act. An NGO can be created only under a Public Trust Act. Diane (2004) in Transfer Agents and Global Network emphasised that globalisation during the 20" century gave rise the importance of NGOs. NGOs have developed to emphasize humanitarian issues, development aid and sustainable development. In the Fifth World Social Forum (2005), more than 1000 NGOs participated to discuss poverty and social issues. A Trust can be registered in one state, but the same has the scope to operate in any number of states. Private Trusts: A private Trust created under governed by the Indian Trust Act of 1882, aims at managing assigned Trust properties for private or religious purposes. A private Trust does not enjoy the privileges and tax benefits that are available for public Trust or NGOs. 7.2.2 NGOs in India: Emergence and Role NGOs or voluntary organisations in India are shaped by a variety of factors; they have been nurtured and threatened in turn as the dominant political outlook has oscillated between liberalism and statism.

Diverse in their functions and purposes, they serve primarily a vast and assorted population of informal workers. A sizeable sum from public and foreign sources is expended by this sector. And yet the sector has 'received surprisingly scanty attention from academic researchers and social analysts. Kaplan (1999) analysed the classical statement of the organisational development approach to development with particular relevance to smaller, indigenous NGOs. Population Foundation of India (1999) emphasised on encouraging the role of Indian NGOs for forming opinion of Panchayati Raj Leaders, local tradition dais, aganwadi workers and private practitioners to participate in planning and implementation. voluntary !organisations tend to be emotional and ideological rather than reflective and rational.

Descriptions of voluntary organisations tend to either praise or denounce them-what is missing is an effort at understanding and interpreting them. Voluntary associations have been seen alternatively as the 'harbingers of silent revolution', 'hand maidens of global imperialism', and 'footnotes in India's development'. If voluntarism was inspired by religion and political ideology, commitment to normative pluralism facilitated its growth. National elites, already steeped in the indigenous cultural conception of society as autonomous of the State, readily embraced normative pluralism.

Their commitment has been manifested in several ways. Formally, the Constitution guarantees the right to form organisations to Indian citizens. In addition to this legal provision, certain practices and norms were developed which promoted voluntary organisations. *First,* from the very outset Indian policy-makers had developed a tradition of consulting social elites and groups. Representative committees were created to secure opinions from various groups in society, and their views were solicited in formulating major domestic policies, even as a centrally planned model of development was adopted. *Second,* voluntary organisations were involved not only in formulating policies, but their help was also sought in implementing programmes. The Planning Commission itself had realised at the outset that the task of development was so large and so complex that the State alone would not be able to accomplish it. Accordingly, the very First Five Year Plan document had camed a plea to voluntary organisations to become involved in the task of development, mainly by implementing government programmes. Appropriate financial provisions were also made for them. Beginning with an allocation of Rs.4 crore in the First Plan, the voluntary sector has been receiving increasing amounts of public funds. In the Eighth Plan it rose to Rs.750 crore and multiplied in subsequent plans. *Finally,* because of the stand of international aid agencies, an extraneous factor has also played a conducive role. In the 1970s, the philosophy and strategy of the international development community began to change. Foreign aid donors started to focus their attention on voluntary organisations as supplementary delivery vehicles for development. They began to channel large amounts of developmental aid to those organisations which worked directly for the poor instead of for the governments. This access to financial resources led to mushrooming of voluntary organisations. The activities of voluntary organisations can be seen in a new way.

Many typologies of voluntary associations have been developed, and the proposed typology makes no radical departure from them. It differs from them only in emphasising the political activities of voluntary associations. The activities can be considered under three heads; developmental, political and catalytic. Developmental, catalytic and political activities are not mutually exclusive, and most voluntary organisations pursue some combination of all three, often in conjunction with each other or as a series of successive steps. However, both voluntary associations themselves and the researchers have shied away from focusing exclusively on political activities.

Community Support

NGOs can obtain community support in two ways.

Encouraging Local Initiatives

The Community Based Voluntary Organisations have the vital responsibilities to encourage local initiatives in terms of mobilisation and enviornment building. The local persons or the stockholders can bring about meaningful change. For example, in Targeted Intervention Programme of National AIDS Control programme (2007), each voluntary organisation has to mobilise local people. The experts while evaluating the programme has to ensure that he local persons, especially various stockholders, have been taken into confidence. The involvement of local people should be ensured by obilisation camps, street plays, awareness camps, sensitisation workshops, and also by involving the local people as volunteers. Voluntary organisations working in the field of Education, Health and on other social development issue have to involve local people in their programmes. Such initiatives need to be documented as success stories, constraints felt and lessons learnt. Voluntary organisations should function on the principles of 'for the people by the people and of the people'. Bhagidari Scheme of the Delhi Government in each Ministry is one of the examples of involving local people in Shrishakti Camps, Gender Resource Centre, and by encouraging Resident Welfare Associations in the local initiatives. The importance of non-governmental organisations in micro/local level intervention can not be ignored. It is well known that Government agencies implement programmes which are planned at the macro level for the benefit of a large section of the population. The NGOs work in isolated pockets, on issues touching the people, at the grassroots.

Enlisting Community Support

As defined by Olivier de Sardan (2005), one of the axioms of community development is that knowledge and experience are vital sources of understanding defines. Chambers (1997) states that local knowledge transfers top down bureaucratic planning, and may even reverse deep rooted patterns of social power and hierarchy. Various examples of grassroots movements can be cited to illustrate their issues, strategies, and nature. The Chipko movement led by Chandi Prasad Bhat in the hills of Uttaranchal galvanised local villagers to protect the felling of trees until an acceptable solution was worked out with the government. Nalini Nayak and Fr. Thomas Kocherry have mobilised coastal fish workers to protect their traditional rights and livelihood. In Madhya Pradesh, the Narmada Bachao Andolan led by Medha Patkar has resulted in sustained peaceful protest by tribals and peasants living in the Narmada Valley-primarily against displacement of tribal people and flooding of their land by a large dam project. The Self-Employed Women's Association (SEWA), a union of women workers in Gujarat, responds to the specific needs of poor self-employed women by providing access to credit and so forth; unlike the other movements, it is not operating in the anti-state space and often "practices a politics of part autonomy from, part engagement with the state. Like the NGOs, these struggle-oriented grassroots movements also form networks to enhance their efficacy. The National Alliance for People's Movements was formed as an umbrella group of more than a hundred grassroots organisations to intervene in the process of economic and political decision making from the perspective of poor and ordinary people.

The National Front for Tribal Self-Rule (NFTSR) represents tribal movements and communities from across the country and successfully spearheaded the movement for extension of self-rule to tribal areas. In addition to these large alliances, activist organisations like the People's Union for Democratic Rights (PUDR) and People's Union for Civil Liberties (PUCL), mostly made up of educated urban progressives, have also played a significant role in supporting grassroots movements through media advocacy and judicial intervention. The majority of the development literature makes a distinction between governmental and non-governmental organisations, particularly with respect to their different roles, functions and objectives. The whole issue, which is associated with NGOs to work together with governmental and inter-governmental institutions, basically rests on their presumed capacity to reach the poor and on the qualities of innovation and flexibility as well as how they view their roles as an active and effective co-partner in articulating more responsibility for a better understanding of some of the macro-policy issues which go beyond the limited local environment in which they work. Nevertheless, *one of the basic* Organisations *for the recent focus on NGOs is that they are perceived as being able to accomplish-u part of the development process that national governments are not able or willing, to do.*

Hence, it is generally recognised that NGOs can have a great potential impact on public policy by interacting with their governments. But it is also important to note that there are vast regional and international differences in relationship between NGOs and governments. For example, NGOs in India are supported and encouraged by the government and are registered with the government and work closely with it. Similarly, NGOs in Africa frequently need to work closely with their governments and try not to antagonise the authorities. On the other extreme, most NGOs in Latin America have historically worked in opposition to the government. In recent years, there is a growing momentum of the emergence of NGOs in Nepal as a major collective actor in development activities, as a result of the changed political scene. Presently, the term has been in use rather quite flexibly to accommodate all the NGOs which would like to be designated as quasi-official in nature because of the close link and support they draw from government establishments. Thus, the nature of the canvas of the NGOs in Nepal is increasingly being recognised as highly relevant to the problems of the rural and urban poor.

However, as the vast majority of poor in Nepal are concentrated in rural areas, the NGOs have a special role to play as agents of change and catalysts of development in the villages, by complementing and supplementing the activities of the government and other developmental agencies. The range and diversity of the growth of NGOs is immense, and the literature and the documentation of their activities are expanding geometrically. However, the evolutionary trends of institutionalised form of such organisations can be traced back to the late 19" and early 20" centuries, particularly in the Western World where the history of social organisation seems to have been largely influenced by the lassies faire movement on the basis of the promulgation of *the* theory relating to minimisation of State-intervention, on the one hand, and dissemination of the concept of 'Volunteerism' in a more planned and organised *way, on the other:* The nineties was an interesting decade in the context of global priorities towards massive expansion of the NGOs, both in terms of the changing direction of the flow of aid funds sector-wise and country-wise. Indeed, social development is the broadest arena in both national as well as international context within which NGOs provide their contribution, which naturally addresses several strategic questions pertinent to prospects, constraints, weaknesses and strategic objectives to future NGO development. Thus, community support in various arenas developed during 19" and 20" century. Since mid 1980s, NGOs have been the primary focus for localised civil society driven interventions in development and this has resulted in marked increase in the number of NGOs operating throughout the developing world.

Community Organisation: 'Community organisation' viewed from a humanitarian' approach to solve the problems of the community, is as old as society itself. But viewed as one of the methods of social work profession it is of very recent origin. There is much ambiguity and vagueness as to the precise meaning of the term 'Community Organisation'. Murray G. Ross (1904) defines community organisation as a "process by which a community identifies its needs or objectives, gives priority to them, develops the confidence and will to work at them, finds resources-internal and external-to deal with them, and in doing so, extends and develops cooperative and collaborative attitudes and practices within the community". In other words, community organisation is a process and a method of organising the community. Its broader definition can be: Community organisation is the process by which the social system of the community provides for integration and adaptation within the community.

This is a process which continues regardless of the work of the community organiser whose function is to initiate, nourish and develop this process. In participating in this process the community organiser should have regard for certain values relating to the forms of social change and the means by which they may be brought about. Community organisation for social welfare (or community welfare organisation) is the process of bringing about and maintaining adjustment between social welfare needs and social welfare resources in a geographical area or a special field of service.

Projects and Innovations

Project-formulation and new innovations are keys to the development of the non-governmental organishtion. The funding agencies at the National and International levels require systematic projects with new innovations. For developing projects new innovative systems, like the following, are developed by various funding agencies.

Expression of Interest: A funding agency, before asking for detailed projects, requires 'Expression of Interest' by the organisation. It deals with the physical, financial and professional capacities of the voluntary organisation. It helps the funding agency in short-listing the organisation.

Executive Summary: For developing innovative projects, an executive summary is desired by the funding agency. It incorporates several points which are scored by the funding agency.

Vision: It incorporates the vision and mission of the voluntary organisation.

Objectives / Outcomes : The long and short-term objectives of the organisation and also about the specific project for which the organisation has applied.

Activities (Proposed): The first and foremost task is to enumerate major and minor activities to be undertaken to achieve the objectives of the project.

Time Schedule / Plan or Time Budget: It is also desired by the funding agency. The activity plan should cover the following details:

Time Plan

Funding-The funding details of recurring and non-recurring expenditure. Funding should also specify the contribution of the organisation applying for the project.

Sustainability-How the programme will sustain itself if the funding is delinked or minimised.

Replicability-What are the issues or important lessons learnt to be replicated by the organisation in other areas or by other funding agency.

Documentation and Dissemination: Project planning should also specify how the process will be documented and how the findings will be disseminated. The funding agency may also provide time for the organisation to present the project proposal or may award the project on the basis of project proposal or may follow additional procedure.

Expert Visit: Some of the funding agencies have started visiting the organisation to understand and review the various capacities and physical infrastructure. The selection of the project is also done on the basis of the expert visit.

Infrastructure and Logistics: Tools and equipments for facilitating project work is also essential.

The implementing agency should have the required infrastructural facilities and logistic support to carry out the project activities. Before initiating the implementation, it becomes necessary to review the existing infrastructural facilities and identify those needed in future. Proper planning is also needed to ensure logistic support.

Periodic Staff Meeting: Staff members and those who are the stockholders meet to review, plan and monitor the programme. Several funding agencies require weekly and monthly review meetings. Such meeting reviews the achievements and the future planning. Such meetings help the grassroots workers to be in tune with the objectives.

Participation of the Community Members: It is to be ensured that all the stockholders in the community are involved in the programme. Their participatory involvement helps in ensuring the success of the programme.

Field and Exposure Visits: Field visits in the project area and exposure visits by the project staff help in implementation and monitoring of the programme.

Monitoring and Evaluation

Monitoring can be defined as a process of measuring, recording, collecting and analysing data on actual implementation of the-programme to identify any deviation from the planned operations. Monitoring can be both internal and external:

- The programme staff monitors the programme in the field by various means. For an effective monitoring system, a plan for the main programme needs to be prepared thoroughly.
- The plan should identify key result areas and how they will be measured. It should also identify linkages of inputs and outputs.

The monitoring process should consist of the following:

- Detecting deviations from the plans.
- Taking corrective action.
- For systematic implementation of any project, monitoring should be done systematically.

Evolving a System of Record Keeping: The first step in monitoring is evolving a system of record keeping. Targeted intervention project implemented by National AIDS Control programme has developed a list for monitoring regular records. It consists of following FACTS:

- F-Factual.
- A-Accurate.

- C-Concise.
- T-Timely.
- S-Simple.

External agencies may also be involved in monitoring. Qualitative and quantitative indicators may be developed for monitoring.

Community Participation: We should secure community participation in monitoring. The continuous feedback should come from the community.

Evaluation: Evaluation is a continuous process aimed at correcting and improving actions in order to render the activities more relevant and effective.

This involves different aspects of implementation of a programme, its relevance, its formulation, its efficiency and effectiveness, its costs and acceptance by the community. Evaluation is expected to identify problems and also possible solutions. Evaluation might be a continuous process or mid-term evaluation or final (summative) evaluation. The process of evaluation should cover the following points:

Ensuring Information Support

- Verify Relevance.
- Assess Adequacy.
- Review Progress.
- Assess Efficiency.
- Assess Effectiveness.
- Assess Impact.

Evaluation of a project may be mid-term or final evaluation. Mid-term evaluation helps, in analysing the progress of the project and the intervention required at that point. The final evaluation is carried out at the end of the project.

Methodology for Evaluation: The methodology of the evaluation of the programme depends upon the purpose of evaluation. For example, health programmes of the Ministry of Health & Family Welfare, implemented through F non-governmental organisations are evaluated each year to recommend the continuation for the next year. It consists of the records evaluation, field-visits and focus group discussions with the various project staff and other community people. The objective of the evaluation is decided on the basis of the programme, objectives and also the financial allocations. It involves success stories, case studies, sample field visits and evaluating the documents and also the capacities of the various staff in relation to their roles and responsibilities. Evaluation helps in the next programme planning, programme designing or using the same interventions in the ongoing programmes. Monitoring and evaluation are essential tools of the non-governmental organisations.

Human Relations and Employees' Welfare

In a technology-driven, fiercely competitive, dynamic and globalised business environment of the 21st century, providing, managing and retaining a quality work force to a corporate organisation is a formidably multifaceted task that an HR professional accomplishes. Moreover, with the businesses growing by gallops across the globe and demand for seasoned HR professionals soaring high, this career has become lucrative and rewarding as handsome monetary returns are commensurate with the stimulating challenges. Human Resource Management or Personnel Management implies the management of human resource or labour, an important input or factor of any organisation or industry, apart from land and capital. The role of an HR professional involves optimally harnessing and utilising the full potential and productivity of the manpower to the best advantage of the industry. Human Resource Management has eventful history of change in nomenclature and nature of functions. It was known as Labour Welfare or Employee Welfare during pre-independence and immediate post independence era. In the wake of subsequent industrialisation, the field grew with the influx of new inputs and technology and came to be renamed as Industrial Relations/IR in our socialism-oriental mixed economy, run by Five-Year Plans. With the liberalisation of Indian economy after 1991 and its entry in integrated world order of competitive economics under the aegis of globalisation, private sector expanded at an exponential pace. Business from foreign shores infiltrated through our porous economic frontiers, new industries cropped up and older ones caught up with the pace of development. Commensurately, infused with greater knowledge and newer skills, HR was recast in the mould of a more reactive and proactive management from the former purely administrative one and acquired its current name. HR manager's multifarious functions broadly include recruiting the right personnel, training them, providing them adequate remuneration. As the pivot of the recruitment process, he/she puts advertisements for job opportunities, screens resumes for short listing potentially right candidates, conducts interviews for selecting those with qualifications suiting the work profile and prepares offer letters specifying the terms and conditions of employment. An HR manager has to be conversant with preparing training programmes in consonance with the specific needs of the company and the job up to the six Sigma Level, currently followed by most companies.

More importantly, he/she has to undertake the mammoth task of managing employees with diverse backgrounds, skill-sets and personalities by understanding their psyche, temper and professional conduct. He/she has to devise strategies for realising the full potential of manpower, like providing them with offers, compensation packages like esops, promotions, job change, rewards, incentives etc. Such efforts are also meant to retain employees, promote their talents, further their motivation and ensure their satisfaction. An HR manager has to be an excellent communicator to be understood well by the employees and to understand and empathise with their grievances, opinions and needs. Further, he/she has to effectively redress their grievances, and complaints and negotiate with the management and employees for an acceptable solution, in accordance with the labour laws and stipulations of agreements between company and employees. Besides, they are engaged with sundry administrative jobs like maintaining employees' records, payroll processing, calculating bonus, leave, etc. Corporate world, though ruthlessly competitive, has to be socially responsible by helping in the socioeconomic progress of underprivileged or underdeveloped sections and promoting the general well-being. Here comes the concept of Corporate Socio-responsibility which HR manager shoulders.

Besides maintaining cordial relations between employees and management, she/he has to society, by preparing and implementing programmes of social welfare like providing education, healthcare and civic amenities to a village. This implies undertaking the construction of schools for children, or imparting professional training to the rural unemployed youth, opening charitable dispensaries for the treatment and medication of the diseased, laying roads, or arranging for sewage system, etc. The HR division thus plays active role in this area.

In such a multi-faceted professional capacity, an HR manager thus acts as a strategic partner and a vital asset to the industry he is associate with. He/she has to be abreast of the developments in the organisations in particular and the business environment in general. He/she also acts as the agent of change, staying alert to the changes in the organisation or the business environment and assiduously responding to them by making suitable customisations in the recruitment process and acclimatising the employees to these changes. Finally, he/she acts as an advocate of employees by effectively addressing their grievances, needs and concerns.

Of late, IT (Information Technology) has been instrumental in facilitating and qualitatively improving the efficiency of the functions of HR. It has fully computerised the entire gamut of HR functions. HR info-system software packages have ensured the proper storage of the vast database of an organisation‘s manpower in a computer system, which can be instantly accessed with the click of a mouse. his has rendered the extraction of data of employees easy and effortless, so that the information can aid the HR manager to assess the relative work efficiency of employees and the need for training an employee to improve certain skills. Automation of routine functions like payroll processing has spared the HR professional from the drudgery of repetitive administration jobs like payroll, gratuity, leave, etc. Therefore, given the sea change brought about in the HR functions by the rapid strides in IT, being computer savvy is the key to successful multi-tasking in HR. Welfare includes anything that is done for the comfort and improvement of employees and is provided over and above the wages. Welfare helps in keeping the morale and motivation of the employees high so as to retain the employees for longer duration.

The welfare measures need not be in monetary terms only but in any kind/forms. Employee welfare includes monitoring of working conditions, creation of industrial harmony through infrastructure for health, industrial relations and insurance against disease, accident and unemployment for the workers and their families. Labour welfare entails all those activities of employer which are directed towards providing the employees with certain facilities and services in addition to wages or salaries. Labour welfare has the following objectives:

1. To provide better life and health to the workers.
2. To make the workers happy and satisfied.
3. To relieve workers from industrial fatigue and to improve intellectual, cultural and material conditions of living of the workers.

The basic features of labour welfare measures are as follows:

1. Labour welfare includes various facilities, services and amenities provided to workers for improving their health, efficiency, economic betterment and social status.
2. Welfare measures are in addition to regular wages and other economic benefits available to workers due to legal provisions and collective bargaining.
3. Labour welfare schemes are flexible and ever-changing.

New welfare measures are added to the existing ones from time to time.

4. Welfare measures may be introduced by the employers, government, employees or by any social or charitable agency.
5. The purpose of labour welfare is to bring about the development of the whole personality of the workers to make a better work force.

The very logic behind providing welfare schemes is to create efficient, healthy, loyal and satisfied labour force for the organisation. The purpose of providing such facilities is to make their work life better and also to raise their standard of living. The important benefits of welfare measures can be summarised as follows:

- They provide better physical and mental health to workers and thus promote a healthy work environment
- Facilities like housing schemes, medical benefits, and education and recreation facilities for workers' families help in raising their standards of living. This makes workers to pay more attention towards work and thus increases their productivity.
- Employers get stable labour force by providing welfare facilities. Workers take active interest in their jobs and work with a feeling of involvement and participation.
- Employee welfare measures increase the productivity of organisation and promote healthy industrial relations thereby maintaining industrial peace.
- The social evils prevalent among the labours such as substance abuse, etc. are reduced to a greater extent by the welfare policies.

Leadership and Group Dynamics

Managers and supervisors frequently face such a dilemma-standards that should be met but aren't for what seems like no apparent reason. What Jeff Lane and other managers/

supervisors sometimes fail to realise is that within every organisation there are often informal group pressures that influence and regulate individual behaviour. Informal groups formulate an implicit code of ethics or an unspoken set of standards establishing acceptable behaviour In Jeff's department, the informal group may have established a norm below that set by the organisation, subtly exercising control over its members regarding the amount of output.

Dynamics of Informal Groups

Informal Groups Almost Always Arise if Opportunities Exist

Often, these groups serve a counter organisational function, attempting to counteract the coercive tendencies in an organisation. If management prescribes production norms that the group considers unfair, for instance, the group's recourse is to adopt less demanding norms and to use its ingenuity to discover ways in which it can sabotage management's imposed standards. Informal groups have a powerful influence on the effectiveness of an organisation, and can even subvert its formal goals. But the informal group's role is not limited to resistance.

The impact of the informal group upon the larger formal group depends on the norms that the informal group sets. So the informal group can make the formal organisation more effective, too. A norm is an implied agreement among the group's membership regarding how members in the group should behave. From the perspective of the formal group, norms generally fall into three categories-positive, negative, and neutral. In other words, norms either support, obstruct, or have no effect on the aims of the larger organisation. For example, it the informal group in Jeff's shop set a norm supporting high output, that norm would have been more potent than any attempt by Jeff to coerce compliance with the standard. The reason is simple, yet profound. The norm is of the group members own making, and is not one imposed upon them. There is a big motivational difference between being told what to do and being anxious to do it. If Jeff had been aware of group dynamics, he might have realised that informal groups can be either his best friend or his worst enemy. He should have been sensitive to the informal groups within his area and he should have cultivated their goodwill and cooperation and made use of the informal group leadership. That is, he should have wooed the leadership of the informal group and enlisted the support of its membership to achieve the formal organisation's aims.

The final effect of his actions might have been positive or negative, depending upon the agreement or lack of it between the informal group and himself. Harnessing the power of informal groups is no easy task. The requirements include: an understanding of group dynamics and, an ability to bring about changes in informal group norms that positively reinforce the formal organisation's goals. As a starting point, managers and supervisors should at least be aware of the reasons behind informal group formation and the properties and characteristics of these groups.

Formation of Informal Work Groups

Individuals are employed by an organisation to perform specific functions. Although the whole person joins an organisation, attention is usually focused on the partial person, the part of the individual doing the job. Because people have needs that extend beyond the work itself, informal groups develop to fill certain emotional, social, and psychological needs. The degree to which a group satisfies its members needs determines the limits within which individual members of the group will allow their behaviour to be controlled by the group.

Sense of Belonging

Several major functions are served by informal groups. For example, the group serves as a means of satisfying the affiliation needs of its members for friendship and support. People need to belong, to be liked, to feel a part of something. Because the informal group can withhold this attractive reward, it has a tool of its own to coerce compliance with its norms.

Identity and Self Esteem

Groups also provide a means of developing, enhancing, and confirming a person's sense of identity and self-esteem. Although many organisations attempt to recognise these higher needs, the nature of some jobs-their technology and environment-precludes this from happening. The long assembly line or endless rows of desks reinforce a feeling of depersonalisation.

Stress Reduction

Another function of groups is to serve as an agent for establishing and testing social reality. For instance, several individuals may share the feeling that their supervisor is a slave driver or that their working conditions are inadequate. By developing a consensus about these feelings, group members are able to reduce the anxiety associated with their jobs.

All for One, One for All

Finally, the informal group serves as a defence mechanism against forces that group members could not resist on their own. Joining forces in a small group makes the members feel stronger, less anxious, and less insecure in the face of a perceived threat. As long as needs exist that are not served by the formal organisation, informal groups will form to fill the gap. Since the group fills many important needs for its members, it influences member behaviour.

Leadership of Informal Work Groups

Informal groups possess certain characteristics that, if understood, can be used to advantage. While many of these characteristics are similar to those of formal organisations, others are unique. One attribute of informal groups is rotational leadership. The informal leader emerges as the individual possessing qualities that the other members perceive as critical to the satisfaction of their specific needs at the moment; as the needs change so does the leader. Only rarely does a single individual possess all of the leadership characteristics needed to fill the various needs of the group. Unlike the formally appointed leader who has a defined position from which to influence others, the informal leader does not possess formal power. If the informal leader fails to meet the group's expectations, he or she is deposed and replaced by another. The informal group's judgment of its leaders tends to be quicker and more cold-blooded than that of most formal groups.

Supervisory Strategies

The supervisor can use several strategies to affect the leadership and harness the power of informal groups. One quick and sure method of changing a group is to cause the leader to change one or more of his or her characteristics. Another is to replace the leader with another person. One common ploy is to systematically rotate out of the group its leaders and its key members. Considering the rotational nature of leadership, a leader may emerge who has aims similar to the formal goals of the organisation. There are problems with this approach, however. Besides the practical difficulties of this, this strategy is blunted by the fact that group norms often persist long after the leader has left the group.

A less Machiavellian approach is for the supervisor to be alert to leaders sympathetic to the supervisor's objectives and to use them toward the betterment of the formal group's effectiveness. Still another method is to attempt to 'co-opt' informal leaders by absorbing them into the leadership or the decision-making structure of the formal group. Co-opting the informal leader often serves as a means of averting threats to the stability of the formal organisation. Remember, though, a leader may lose favour with the group because of this association with management, and group members will most likely select another leader.

Informal Work Group Communication

Another characteristic of the informal group is its communications network. The informal group has communications processes that are smoother and less cumbersome than those of the formal organisation. Thus its procedures are easily changed to meet the communication needs of the group. In the informal group, a person who possesses information vital to the group's functioning or well-being is frequently afforded leadership status by its members. Also, the centrally located person in the group is in the best position to facilitate the smooth flow of information among group members. Knowing about informal group communication the supervisor can provide a strategically placed individual with information needed by the group. This not only enhances the stature of this individual perhaps elevating him or her to a leadership position but also provides an efficient means of distributing information. Providing relevant information to the group will also help foster harmony between the supervisor and the informal group. By winning the cooperation of informal group leaders the supervisor will most likely experience fewer grievances and better relationships.

Informal Group Cohesiveness

A third characteristic of informal groups is group cohesiveness-the force that holds a group together. Group cohesiveness varies widely based on numerous factors-including the size of the group dependence of members upon the group achievement of goals status of the group and management demands and pressures. For example group cohesiveness increases strongly whenever the membership perceives a threat from the outside. This threat produces the high anxiety that strong group cohesiveness can help reduce. If the supervisor presses the group to conform to a new organisational norm that Is viewed as a threat to the security needs of group members The group will become more unified in order to withstand the perceived threat. Thus management can limit its own effectiveness by helping to increase the group's cohesiveness. With the passing of the threat the group tends to lose its cohesiveness. Perhaps paradoxically the most dangerous time for group cohesion is when things are going well. Supervisors can use the factors that affect group cohesiveness to increase their own effectiveness.

Decision Making Process Involvement

For instance a supervisor can involve the informal group

members in the decision-making process. Input from group members will not only reduce their feeling of alienation but also improve communication between the supervisor and subordinates thereby reducing potential conflict. Where group participation in decision making is not practical the supervisor should carefully explain the reasons to play down what might be seen as a threat to the group. In some cases the supervisor may want to increase the groups cohesiveness deliberately devising situations that put one group into competition with another. If this gambit is carefully controlled the solidarity that results may bring a higher level of performance. The danger of this strategy is that the supervisor may be unable to control the reaction of the group. The ploy could backfire bringing competition and dissension within the group.

Informal Group Norms or Values (Unspoken Rules)

The final characteristic of informal groups is the establishment of the groups norms (values). As we discussed earlier, norms keep a group functioning as a system instead of a collection of individuals. Norms are of great importance to the informal group in controlling behaviour and measuring the performance of members. Because norm (values) violations threaten a group's existence, departures from the norm usually carry severe sanctions. The members must either conform or sever their group affiliation. The latter action is unlikely, especially if the individual values group membership to satisfy certain needs.

Two Points are Important to Note About the Norms of Informal Groups

First, where both formal and informal norms exist, the informal norms transcend the formal. At moments when norms conflict with organisational objectives, organisational effectiveness suffers. Second, members of an informal group may be unaware that the norms of the group influence their behaviour. Norms are particularly potent because without knowing it members would not even think of acting otherwise-norms are that ingrained into their behaviour pattern.

The Role of Voluntary Action

As India has the largest population of poor people, community development has assumed high priority. The initial programme aimed at upliftment of the rural poor, covered agriculture, animal husbandry, roads, health, education, housing, employment, social and cultural activities. However, food security being the main cause of concern, agriculture received significant attention. In 1957, a three-tier-system of rural local Government, called.Panchayati Raj. (Rule by Local Councils) was established. These were Gram Panchayat (Village level), Panchayat Samiti (Block level) and Zilla Parishad (District level). The aim was to decentralise the process of decision making and encourage people.s participation. As the programme could not fulfil the expectations of the rural poor, the Integrated Rural Development Programme (IRDP) was introduced in 1979, with specific focus on the weaker sections of the society. By mid eighties, the Government was able to meet the minimum needs of the poor, which included elementary education, health, water supply, roads, electrification, housing and nutrition. In 1987, the Planning Commission decided to consider block as the basic unit for development planning. The task of planning at the district level was entrusted to the District Planning and Development Council which had wider representation of the society. Panchayati Raj reforms were introduced through the 73rd Constitutional Amendment to facilitate planning at the micro-level and to strengthen the Gram Sabha (village assembly).

The Government of India has also been encouraging voluntary action to mobilise the rural people. Several initiatives of the non-government organisations in the last two decades have had significant impact on the development. NGOs such as BAIF Development Research Foundation are promoting sustainable livelihood through dairy husbandry, water resource management, wastelands development and various income generation activities in several states. Farmers in several states have established cooperatives for processing sugarcane, oil-seeds, milk, fruits and vegetables. With professional management and application of modern technologies, these organisations have brought economic stability and eliminated exploitation by intermediary traders. To strengthen people.s organisations, Self Help Groups (SHGs), comprising of poor families have been promoted under the Ninth Five Year Plan (1997-2002). It is only the peoples initiatives and involvement which can sustain the development. The government and political power have the will to support peoples movement and this should promote sustainable rural development in India.

Problems of the Poor

Poverty in Poverty in India is judged by the income generated by the family. Unemployment and underemployment are the major causes of rural poverty. The other factors are small land holdings, harsh agro-climatic conditions, poor infrastructure and limited opportunities for rural industrial development, poor health care, illiteracy, social suppression, addiction to alcohol and exploitation by vested interests. Land is the major resource in India, which provides livelihood to the rural population. According to a survey about 11.25% of the rural families are landless and among the land holders, over 69.35% own less than 1 ha (marginal farmers) and 21.25% own between 1 and 2 ha (small farmers). Water is another critical resource required to enhance the agricultural production. Out of the total arable area of 169 million ha, only 28% area is under irrigation and the rest is dependent on rains, where hardly one crop can be grown in a year. About 40% of the cropping area is located in low rainfall regions where the employment opportunity is hardly for 40 to 50 days in a year and crops generally fail twice in five years. Decline in many traditional occupations and poor institutional infrastructures have further reduced job opportunities. Thus about 90% of the rural population, who are deprived of adequate land holding have to look for other means of livelihood for their survival. Livestock is another important natural resource owned by the poor. Generally the rural families keep 1-2 cows or buffaloes for milk, a pair of bullocks for farming and a few sheep, goats and poultry for supplementary income. Although fodder is in scarcity, most of the poor families maintain large herds and let them graze on common lands. Dairy husbandry has good scope, as there is good demand for milk. However, most of the important breeds of cattle and buffaloes are genetically eroded and about 80-85% of the livestock are unproductive and cause undue pressure on forest resources while the rural poor are unable to take advantage of these animals. It is feasible to make sustainable use of these natural resources through application of appropriate technologies and use of idle labour. Apart from inadequate earning for livelihood, the rural people also suffer from poor health arising from starvation, lack of immunisation, hygiene and sanitation. Over 25% villages do not have year-round supply of drinking water and about 75% of the potable water sources are polluted. Consumption of polluted water is the main source of illness particularly during the rainy season. Most of the villages have no drainage and sanitation and less than 10% of the rural people use latrines.

Medical and immunisation services do not reach remote villages. Illiteracy in rural areas is high particularly among women, varying from 55% to 75%. This has a direct bearing on the population growth, child health and education. With the annual birth rate of 28 per 1000, as compared to 23 in Asia, the family size has been growing without any addition to the income. Unable to meet the growing needs, the rural poor have to depend on money lenders, to meet their emergencies and fall into the debt trap. They often try to forget their problems by consuming alcohol.

While some migrate to cities, others live in chronic poverty. They lose confidence in others as well in their ability to live a decent life. This is a vicious cycle. The major factor influencing the successful implementation of rural development in India is motivation of the poor families to ensure their active participation. Development of suitable peoples organisations is also necessary to avail the benefits of various schemes, particularly by the illiterate poor. To ensure peoples involvement in the development process and to take them into confidence, they should be involved in the programme, right from the stage of planning.

Several innovative programmes implemented on a pilot scale have shown that many rational suggestions made by even the poor people can be easily implemented to produce good results. Such an approach demands flexibility in the programme. The target families should be motivated to assume the responsibility of implementing the programme, while the implementing agencies should play the role of a catalyst. In this task of integrated rural development, voluntary agencies can play an important role (Sachidananda, 1988). The voluntary organisations or non-government organisations (NGOs) in general focus their voluntary action and service to tackle the problems of the common people or to help them face their challenges.

The main characteristic of voluntary agencies is human-touch. Organisations with strong voluntarism and professionalism can implement the programme efficiently. Dedication of the volunteers and staff, their relationship with the community, flexibility in the programme, innovative approaches to solve the problems can result in greater success. Agencies having deep roots in rural areas can serve the community more effectively (Paul Choudhary, 1990). It was only during the seventies that the government recognised the role of voluntary agencies in supplementing governments effort in rural development.

Prior to this, the NGOs formed by religious institutions and enlightened public were involved in operating hospitals and educational institutions. With assistance from international donor agencies, the Ministry of Agriculture formed an independent organisation called. Freedom from Hunger Campaign to support the voluntary organisations involved in rural development. This Organisation was reorganised and renamed as Peoples Action for Development-India (PAD-I). PAD-I was merged with Council for Advancement of Rural Technology in 1986 and renamed as Council for Advancement of Peoples Action and Rural Technology (CAPART). Since then, CAPART has been providing financial assistance to voluntary agencies engaged in rural development. In the last two decades, several initiatives of the nongovernment organisations have had significant impact on the development. Widespread success of these initiatives have now encouraged many state governments to launch schemes to promote peoples participation and several centrally sponsored schemes have stipulated the development of community based organisations to plan and implement the programme. With better opportunities for promoting self-employment through investment in agriculture and micro-enterprise, facilities were created for availing soft loans from banks and other financial institutions.

The Reserve Bank of India issued guidelines to all the bankers not to insist on collateral security up to Rs.25,000 drawn by the poor for investment in development activities. As a result, over Rs.250 billion was distributed as rural credit in 1995-96, of which 50% amount was from the cooperatives and the rest from other banking institutions. Nevertheless, as the formal banking operations were not convenient for many villagers because of their rigidity, distance and high cost of operation, several innovative banking institutions have been established by the NGOs.

Peoples Initiatives for Progress

Farmers in several states have established cooperatives for processing sugarcane, oil-seeds, milk, fruits and vegetables. With professional management and application of modern technologies, these organisations have brought economic stability and eliminated exploitation by intermediary traders. Encouragement is being given to strengthen such organisations throughout the country. Under a nationwide programme for water resource development, involvement of NGOs as facilitators and formation of water users organisations have been encouraged to prepare the microlevel plan and implement the project directly. This programme has made a significant impact on the supply of drinking water and greater awareness is being created on the need to conserve water and energy resources.

There is scope for promoting such peoples organisations in other fields as well to develop necessary infrastructure required to enhance economic prosperity. Considering the need for promoting peoples initiatives and local organisations, Self Help Groups, comprising of poor families have been promoted under the Ninth Five Year Plan (1997-2002), through the Swarnajayanti Gram Swarojgar Yojana (SGSY) in 1999. SHGs consisting of 10-20 members belonging to backward socioeconomic status encourage the participants to meet regularly to collect their savings and disburse it as loan to needy members.

REFERENCES

Cameiro, Robert L ed, 1967, The Evolution of Sociology: *Selections from Herbert Spencer's Principles of Sociology,* Chicago: University of Chicago Press.

Campbell, Donald, 1971, "Methods for Experimenting Society: (Paper presented at the meeting of the American Psychological Association, Washington, D.C.: September.

MacRae, Duncan, and James Wilde, *1979, Policy Analysis for Public* Decisions, N. Scituate, Ma.: Duxbury.

Rosenberg, Bernard, Israel Gerver, and F. William Howton, 1971, *Mass Society in Crisis: Social Problems and Social Pathology.* 2nd ed, New York: Macmillan, 1st edition. 1964.

Weber, Max, 1947: *The Theory of Social and Economic Organisation,* trans. by A.M. Henderson and T. Persons, New York: Oxford University Press.

Bibliography

Basu, Amrita (2012). *Two Faces of Protest: Contrasting Modes of Women's Activism in India.* Berkeley: University of California Press.

Bonner, Arthur (2010). *Averting the Apocalypse: Social Movement in India Today.* Durham: Duke University Press.

Calman, Leslie J. (1992). *Toward Empowerment: Women and Movement Politics in India.* Boulder, CO; Westview Press, pp 21-46.

Clark, John (2011). *Democratising Development: The Role of Voluntary Organisations.* London: Earthscan Publications.

Elliott, Mabel A. and Merrill, Francis E., *Social Disorganisation,* Harper and Brothers, New York, 1950.

Erikson, Kai T 2000, "Notes on the Sociology of Deviance", *Social Problems, 9,*311 (Spring), reprinted in Howard S. Becker. ed., *The Other Side,* Glencoe: The Free Press, 1964, pp. 9-15.

Faris, Robert E.L, and Warren Dunhan, 1997, *Mental Disorders in Urban Areas: An Ecological Study of Schizophrenia and Other Psychoses,* Chicago: University of Chicago Press.

Faris, Robert EL, 2007, *Chicago School 1920-1932,* San Francisco: Chandler.

Fuller, Richard C. and Myres, Richard R., "The Natural History of a Social Problem", *American Sociological Review,* 1941.

Garfinkel, Harold, 1995, "Conditions of Successful Degradation Ceremonies", *American Journal of Sociology,* 61, 5 (March), pp. 420-425.

Garson, G. David, 2006, "From Policy Science to Policy Analysis-A Quarter Century of Progress", in William N. Dunn, ed. *Policy Analysis: Perspectives, Concepts and Methods,* Greenwich, Ct.: J.A.I. Press.

Gillin, J.L., Dittmen, C.G. Colbert, R.J. and Kastler, N.M., *Social Problems,* The Times of India Press, Bombay, 1995.

Glass, D.V., 1990, "The Application of Social Research," *British Journal of Sociology,* 1(1).

Goddard, Henry H., 1994, *The Kallikak Family,* New York: the Macmillan Company.

Gouldner, A.W., 2006, "Explorations in Applied Social Science" *Social Problems,* 111 (3).

Gunther W. Rammling, 2005. *The Sociology' of Karl Mannheim,* Routledge and Kegan Paul, London, p. 128.

Habennas, Jurgen, 2001, *Toward a Rational Society,* London:" Heinemann.

Hansman, H. (2000). 'The role of non-profit enterprise', *Yale Law Journal* 89, pp 835-901.

Hardgrave, Robert L., Jr and Stanley A. Kochanek (2006). *India: Government and Politics in a Developing Nation.* San Diego: Harcourt Brace.

Hawkesworth, M.E., 2008, *Theoretical Issues in Policy Analysis 'New* York: State University of the New York Press.

Healy, Paul, 2006, "Interpretive Policy Inquiry: A Response to the Limitations of the Received View", *Policy Sciences,* 19: 381-396.

Henderson, Charles, 1999, *Introduction to the study of the Dependent, Defective and Delinquent Classes and Their Social Treatment,* Boston: D.C. Heath.

Hermon, Abbon P., *An Approach to Social Problems, Ginn,* Boston, 2009.

Heworth, L, 2010, "The Experimenting Society: Devey and Jorden", *Ethics,* 71: 27-40.

Hill, Michael, 2010, *Understanding Social Policy,* Oxford: Basil Blackwell.

Jain, Devaki (2006).'Struggle against power: Notes on Indian political behaviour', *World Politics* 7, pp. 393-96.

Jhunjhunwala, Bharat (2006). 'Voluntary work as countervailing power,' *Economic and Political Weekly* 21.

Kahn, Robert L., 2004, *Organisational Stress: Studies in Role Conflict and Ambiguity,* New York: John Wiley.

Karat, Prakash (2004). 'Action groups/voluntary organisations: A factor in imperialist strategy', *The Marxist,* April-June, pp 19-54.

Kasona. George, 2010, *The Powerful Consumer: Psychological Studies of the American Economy,* New York: McGraw-Hill.

Kershaw, David, el al., 1996, *Final Report of the New Jersey Graduated Work Incentive Experiment,* New York: Academic Press, 4 Vols.

Kinsey Alfred, et. al., *Sexual Behaviour in the Human Male,* W.B. Saunders Co., Philadelphia, 1998.

Kisuse, John I., 2002, "Societal Reaction to Deviance: Problems of Theory and Method", *Social Problems, 9* (Winter), pp. 247-256.

Kitsuse, John I., 2000, "The New Conception of Deviance and Its Critics", in Walter R. Gove, ed., *The Labelling of Deviance: Evaluating a Perspective,* 2nd ed., Baverly Hills, California: Sage.

Kitz, Elihu, and Paul F. Lazarsfeld, 1995, *Personal Influence,* Glencoe, III.: The Free Press.

Kochanek, Stanley A. (1994). *Business and Politics in India.* Berkeley: University of California Press.

Kolb, William L., "The Impingement of Moral Values on Sociology" in *Social Problems,* October, 1994.

Kothari, Smitu (2013). 'Social movements and the redefinition of democracy' in Philip Oldenburg (ed.), *India Briefing.* Boulder, CO: Westview Press, p. 142.

Laskin Richard (ed.), *Social Problems,* Mcgraw Hill Co., New York, 2004.

Lasswell, Harold, 2001, "The Policy Orientation", in Haroid Lasswell and Daniel Lerner, eds. *The Policy Sciences: Recent Developments in Science and Method, Stanford:* Stanford University Press.

Lemert, Edwin M., 2001, *Social Pathology A Systematic Approach to the Theory of Sociopathic Behaviour,* New York: McGraw-Hill.

Myrdal, Gunnar, 2008, *Asian Drama: An Inquiry into the Poverty of Nations,* Harmondsworth: Fenguin, 3 Vols.

Pandey, Shashi Ranjan (2011). *Community Action far Social Justice: Grassroots Organisation in India.* New Delhi: Sage Publications.

Reinhardt, James M., Meadows Paul and Gillette, John M., *Social Problems and Social Policy,* American Book Co., New York, 2001.

Robert K. Merton and Nisbet, R. 1996. *Contemporary Social Problems:* Harcourt, Brace: New York, p. 26.

Rubington, Earl, and Martin S. Weinberg, eds., 1997, *The Study of Social Problems: Five Perspectives,* New York: Oxford University Press.

Sachidananda and B.B. Mandal, 1995. *Industrialisation and Social Disorganisation:* Concept Publications: New Delhi, p. 22.

Shah, Dinesh (2005). 'Voluntary agencies in the seventh plan', *Voluntary Action* 27, nos. 9-10, p. 259.

Viswanath, Vanita (2011) *Non-governmental Organisations and imen's Development in South Asia: A Comparative Analysis*. Boulder, CO: Westview Press.

Waller, Willard, "Social Problems and the Mores", *American Sociological Review,* (1), 2006.

Weber, Max, 2007: *The Theory of Social and Economic Organisation,* trans. by A.M. Henderson and T. Persons, New York: Oxford University Press.

Weinberg, Kirson, S. *Social Problems in Our Times,* Prentice Hall Inc., Englewood Cliffs, New Jersey, 2010.

Whitebead, Alfred North, 2011, *The Aims of Education*, New York: New American Library.

Whyte, William F., *Street Corner Society,* University of Chicago Press, Chicago, 2005.

Index